HACKATHON

A FIELD GUIDE TO IDEATING, LEADING AND WINNING

Alvin Chia

Marshall Cavendish
Business

To Gladys, Mama and Papa,
who made me who I am today.

Published by Marshall Cavendish Business
An imprint of Marshall Cavendish International

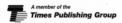
A member of the
Times Publishing Group

Other Marshall Cavendish Offices:
Marshall Cavendish Corporation. 99 White Plains Road, Tarrytown NY 10591-9001, USA • Marshall Cavendish International (Thailand) Co Ltd. 253 Asoke, 12th Flr, Sukhumvit 21 Road, Klongtoey Nua, Wattana, Bangkok 10110, Thailand • Marshall Cavendish (Malaysia) Sdn Bhd, Times Subang, Lot 46, Subang Hi-Tech Industrial Park, Batu Tiga, 40000 Shah Alam, Selangor Darul Ehsan, Malaysia

National Library Board, Singapore Cataloguing-in-Publication Data

Name(s): Chia, Alvin.
Title: Hackathons unboxed : a field guide to ideating, leading and winning / Alvin Chia ; with foreword by Neal Cross.
Description: Singapore : Marshall Cavendish Business, [2017]
Identifier(s): OCN 1004506935 | ISBN 978-981-4779-25-8 (paperback)
Subject(s): LCSH: Creative ability in business. | Technological innovations. | New products. | Workshops.
Classification: DDC 650.1—dc23

Book design by Bernard Go Kwang Meng
Cover design by Anthony Lew

Printed in Singapore by Markono Print Media Pte Ltd

CONTENTS

FOREWORD

THE BIGGEST ENEMY of corporations is the silo mentality that "I know best" – this egotistical statement that senior executives rely on. In fairness, their deep knowledge of their industry and role has worked well for many years. But the world is changing. There are new ways of execution, new potential partnerships, and more importantly, new competitors who are smarter and faster than the incumbents.

As I have often said, the problem isn't that banking needs to go digital – it's that digital is getting into banking. At DBS Bank, we embarked upon a dramatic path to become world-class. Rather than focus just on innovation, we felt it was important to provoke a cultural transformation and become a leader in our industry. Using common tools like design thinking and lean start-up structures, we have kindled highly engaging hackathons, where we partner banking executives with start-ups, students and our clients to define the future of Asian finance. Going through this, we realised how powerful a tool the customer journey is for reducing the amount of "I know best", to get laser-focused on the exact needs of our clients.

We have evolved our methodology since we started. The DBS hackathon is now a three-day event that brings together the top talents from our bank and some of the brightest minds from the FinTech world. We have even extended the power of hackathons to our undergraduate interns through the UNI.CORN programme, where students can take a bite of the real challenges that banks face today.

Our daring towards exploring the unknown has won us fans both locally and around the world. Amongst the accolades we have received, being voted the world's best digital bank in 2016 by Euromoney is one of the best testimonies of how well the digital mindset has been propagated and entrenched – through the hackathon! – within DBS Bank.

Hackathons Unboxed encapsulates the spirit of all that we have pulled off. Alvin has put together a highly practical field guide to help you replicate the magic behind the DBS hackathons we conduct. Whether you are an aspiring hacker, or a hackathon organiser yourself, I'm sure you'll learn something valuable from this book.

Neal Cross
Managing Director and Chief Innovation Officer
DBS Bank

INTRODUCTION

ON MY FIRST day at DBS Bank in Singapore, I found myself reporting for work at Changi Airport, waiting for my new colleagues, whom I had met briefly during the interviews.

The duo who greeted me were David Beath and Darren Yeo, from the DBS Innovation Group. After a warm handshake and a short welcome, I was handed two bags. One contained a laptop, the other contained research materials to "get me started". I had no idea what to expect. With that, we boarded our flight and jetted off to Jakarta, where I would have my first taste of a DBS hackathon.

The next three days exposed me to the hackathon methodology. I had the good fortune of being the table facilitator for an amazingly talented team from DBS Indonesia. The experience, as David aptly put it, was an emotional rollercoaster ride: we started off with a high on the first day, before sinking low towards the end of the second day, but came back strongly, ending on a high after the pitch.

The winning team took home cash prizes and an opportunity to build a first-in-market digital product for the bank. Besides the positive vibes and friendships forged, the hackathon left me with a lasting impression, kickstarted my tenure in the best way possible, and also gave me three key takeaways that would form the foundation of this book:

1. Disruption is happening

With smartphones opening new worlds of possibilities, technology has allowed first and fast movers to seize the initiative. In the finance sphere, incumbents are up against the likes of Alibaba (with its Alipay and Ant Financial) and Tencent (WeBank, Wechat Pay, Tenpay). Outside of the banking world, ride-hailing app such as Uber and Grab are also quickly disrupting the transportation market. But remember, it is practices like Human-Centred Design (HCD), experimentation and rapid prototyping that made these disruptions possible. And these practices are open to all.

2. Business-As-Usual (BAU) churns out the usual

How are businesses responding to these disruptions? Very often, we hear that it is BAU. We do certain things because they've been done this way for the past decades. However, with rapid changes expected in the years ahead, BAU simply cannot respond to customers' needs. From budgeting cycles to the layers of approval required and a long release backlog, it could take years before your new product reaches your customers. BAU further stifles creativity as teams seek to provide incremental growth based on tested and proven strategies – far behind the 10x growth that disruptors are getting.

3. Enter hackathons

As the world seeks new ways to answer these disruptions, we've chosen hackathons. Hackathons are intense events in which bright minds are brought together in teams to tackle a business challenge over a very short period of time. Picture a room crammed full of people brimming with ideas. They will spend the next three days of their lives there, with nothing but full-hearted dedication to cracking a problem. Ambitious challenge statements provoke tension and keep energy high. The idea is that the enormous competition and pressure will exponentially incubate more new concepts than normal circumstances.

But do hackathons work?

Most certainly. Just ask Facebook. Some of its most familiar features were born of hackathons – the Like button, Facebook chat, and even Facebook videos. It is no wonder that the company swears by them.

Hackathons have spawned successful startups too. At a New York City hackathon in 2010, two participants successfully prototyped a group messaging app. They went on to found a company known as GroupMe, which was later acquired by Skype for US$85 million. Back in Singapore, we have Carousell, an app which allows users to trade new and used items. It was conceived at a 2012 hackathon, and has now become one of the largest mobile marketplaces in the region.

If you are surprised that such game-changers could be conceived within a short span of days, you are not alone. It is no wonder that many newcomers have found themselves addicted to hackathons.

Start the corporate revolution

Catching on, established companies have turned to hackathons to bring out the inner startup in their staff. With decades of history, these companies tend to accumulate volumes of standard-operating procedures (SOPs) in addition to the

A hackathon in
full swing

BAUs which serve them well. But the rigid structure can also hinder the initiative and agility of the company. Hackathons offer a safe space to rewrite the rules, as companies don't need to abandon their businesses just to innovate.

Hackathons are not limited to Silicon Valley companies seeking to iterate new software. IDEO, a leader in design thinking, first tested the make-a-thon format in 2012. They brought together London's industrial designers, architects, and 3D printing experts to prototype physical products, such as a rear bicycle light to detect when traffic behind was moving too close, all in a bid to solve social challenges.

For British Airways, the sky was literally the limit, when they took their 2017 travel technology hackathon onboard an A380 jet plane. Called Hack Horizon, engineers, designers and entrepreneurs retraced the footsteps of travellers from Regal Hotel in Hong Kong, up the airplane, before finally testing their solutions at London's Heathrow airport. What this means is that hackathon-style prototyping can be brought to any industry, to address any problem.

Exposing staff to a start-up culture during a hackathon can also be a first step towards creating a new "maker" mindset within the company. For instance, within DBS Bank, we have used hackathons as a talent development tool, by pairing staff with entrepreneurs to solve problems. Since 2015, the programme has gone through multiple iterations, reaching thousands of staff. Hackathons are also an important tool for helping us reach the Big Hairy Audacious Goal (BHAG) of transforming DBS into a 22,000-person startup.

Hackathons can also be used as a method to identify talent outside the organisation. One such example is DBS's recently unveiled Hack2Hire programme, where we seek to hire up to 100 software developers from a two-day hackathon. This programme has been a huge success, with business units reaching out pro-actively to bring these new hires into their departments.

Another example would be DBS Innovation Group's very own UNI.CORN Management Internship, where we put up to 60 aspiring interns through a 24-hour Idea Smash hackathon to handpick 24 of them for a three-month internship.

There are also external hackathons, which crowdsource talent outside the organisation to solve problems. These can be for new product ideas or to tackle challenges as grand as those of an entire country. The Singapore government has organised multiple hackathons on nation-wide concerns such as improving public transport and coping with the challenges of an ageing population. One of the first hackathons ever held locally, CODE::XTREMEAPPS:: (CXA), organised by IMDA (Infocomm Media Development Authority), recently reached its 10th anniversary milestone in 2016.

But it doesn't become a hackathon just because you call it one

Having read so far, you may still be sceptical that such success can apply to your company.

It is important to acknowledge upfront that not all hackathons succeed. In fact many fail to produce any earth-shattering ideas. It is easy for critics to pounce on those that don't solve real problems. However, much of this is due to misunderstanding about what hackathons really are.

Contrary to popular belief, hackathons don't simply happen - they require careful orchestration. We don't create magic by tacking the hackathon label onto conventional "brainstorming" sessions or "change management" sessions, when everything else within them is done the same old way. If the experience does not seem a clean break from the usual, participants will imagine it to be just a fad.

The First Hackathons

Like the invention of the telephone, there does not seem to have been one person who can lay claim to the hackathon. The first recorded hackathons occurred within weeks of each other.

In June 1999, a group of developers working on the open-source operating system OpenBSD came together in Calgary. About a week later, another group of developers came together to a write software for the Palm V personal digital assistant, which was handheld.

And so, the hackathon as we know it was born!

Even worse is when participants simply go through the motions – definitely *not* what we want. I've witnessed many hackathons run aground because the participants were bored and eventually left more demoralised than when they started – all huge red flags.

We stress that a tick-the-boxes mentality is the opposite of what we are trying to achieve. The most important thing is embodying the spirit of the hack, by being willing to pierce boundaries.

As a start, senior management will have to lead by being front and centre. This is easy to say, but harder to achieve. Due to the unfamiliar nature of the hackathon methodology, the tendency is for inertia to set in and participants reverting to their old ways of working. Unless leaders actively walk the talk by investing, time, energy and resources in the hackathon, and by encouraging outlandish, even crazy-sounding ideas, it may be hard to inspire a breakthrough.

Remember also that finishing a hackathon doesn't signal the end of the innovation journey. For many organisations, this is just the beginning. Ideas born of the hack need follow-through, for instance, by securing a place in formal work plans. Otherwise the sparks that you have created may fizzle out all too easily!

How to use this book

Hackathons Unboxed is written as a field guide for either planning, conducting or participating in a hackathon. Regardless what role you play, you are bound to find the knowledge shared in this book useful and applicable. The ten chapters will guide you through a typical three-day hackathon:

Chapter 1. Plan-A-Hack lays out the basic tenets of running a hackathon from the logistical perspective. From who to invite, to a ten-day countdown prior to the event, understand what goes behind the scenes to bring about a successful hackathon.

Chapter 2. Insights Preparations discusses the research work that is done prior to the hackathon. To make the best of the three-day event, organisers typically commission research agencies to uncover insights and personas (customer profiles) to help the teams jumpstart the process.

Chapter 3. Generating High Energy shares how the best hackathon organisers take care of their participants to ensure that everyone is at their best during the hackathon.

Chapters 4, 5 and 6 on Human-Centred Design (HCD) take you on a crash course to understand how HCD tools can be used in fieldwork to better understand the customer, land insights, and build towards the eventual ideation where concepts are developed to solve the customer's needs.

Chapters 7 and 8 on Prototyping shed light on how concepts are experimented on to ensure that they pass the test of customer desirability, going from low-fidelity prototyping to mid- and high-fidelity prototypes.

Chapter 9. Facilitation and Mentorship will discuss the various facilitation and mentorship roles within the hackathon itself – from the main facilitators to the table facilitators and the business mentors – and how they help guide the teams.

Chapter 10. Pitching and Judging is where everything comes together. All the hard work, sweat and tears culminates in a five-minute pitch where the best team in chosen. Tips on pitching, including a slide-by-slide breakdown of what is expected, will ensure you deliver the best pitch ever.

Being an innovator-at-heart, I would advise you to ignore the fixed sequence in which the book is arranged. Creating a

3-Day Hackathon: Programme

DAY 1

DAY 2

DAY 3

1. Opening

2. Insights sharing

3. Pre-fieldwork
Persona
hypothesis
Stakeholder
mapping
Research planning

4. Fieldwork
Interview
Theme
Insights

Homework:
Interview (part 2)

1. Ideation
Boundary
questions
Brainstorming
Conceptualising

2. Prototyping
Experimenting
with low-fidelity
Experimenting
with mid-fidelity

**3. Business
mentoring**

Homework:
Pitch prep

1. Pitch prep

2. Pitch

3. Judging

4. Closing

customer-centric solution is not a linear process. The book's chapters mirror the agenda of a typical three-day hackathon, but do not let this stop you from jumping straight to the chapter that interests you most.

Now if you are ready for your hackathon adventure, let's go!

CHAPTER 1

PLAN-A-HACK

LET'S GET TO business proper. Running a hackathon is no mean feat – and by that I mean that it can be both a logistical nightmare and a hotbed for bad press. I have seen spectacular hacks that uplifted the reputation of the organisers and also those that were doomed to fail from the very beginning. To stay clear of the latter, I have some very practical advice for both aspiring and existing hackathon organisers.

Who to invite?

Deciding who to invite will help you get the first step right. Broadly speaking, there are three categories of invitees to have at your event.

The hackers/participants

Depending on what you want to get done, how much resources you have, the logistical difficulties and cost involved, start by determining how many hackers you want at the event.

From the official standpoint, I always recommend hackathon teams to be in groups of six. There are some good reasons for this. Based on research in behavioural studies, teams of six are the most productive as no one can freeload and there is almost always work for everyone to do. You could also sub-divide the team into two working units, with equal number of hackers on parallel work streams.

If the teams get any larger, there will almost certainly be members who are less engaged. From a team culture standpoint, having one disengaged member can spell trouble as this is all it takes to bring down the team's overall morale and productivity. On the other hand, smaller teams are also not ideal as they won't have enough manpower and brainpower to plough through all the activities required in the three-day hack.

How many teams to have at the hackathon really depends on the resources available. I've conducted hackathons of all sizes, but generally speaking, I would invite at least four teams to ensure a healthy level of competition. Having a room of 25 also ensures that there is a good amount of buzz and chatter, to give the teams a taste of the hustle and bustle of hackathons.

As a seasoned corporate hackathon organiser, I find that the difficulty doesn't lie in assembling 25 hackers. The tough part is getting their commitment and unwavering support. As a rule of thumb, those who cannot commit three days from their busy schedule should not be participating. I've seen hackers walking in and out during the hack, which is

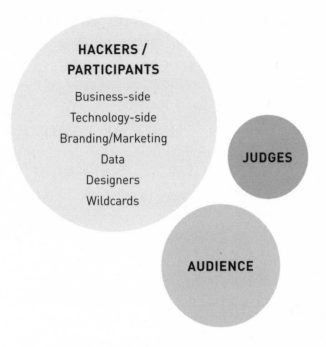

disruptive to say the least. Sending delegates or alternate members is also not ideal as we typically select participants based on their exact profile, which will be different if a replacement takes over.

You might then ask, who are good hackers? For a team of six, I would populate it with one business domain expert, one from the technology side, one from branding/marketing, one data scientist, one user experience (UX) designer, and lastly, one wildcard. This, of course, is a dream list. We usually make do with what we have, but the non-negotiable ones are business experts and designers; the rest are good to have.

1. **Business-side:** Depending on the challenge of the day, if we're solving a digital payments

challenge, it might be someone from the e-business team. If we are cracking an insurance challenge, it might be someone from the bancassurance arm of the bank.

2. **Technology-side:** Someone with the ability to make high-level estimates as to what is needed to get things done and how much it might potentially cost. The technology folks can also be really good at digital prototyping as they typically come with some tech know-how.

3. **Branding/marketing:** Your go-to person if you want to make sure that your product sells. From crafting a one-liner tagline to an acute understanding of what the customers needs, your marketing expert is almost critical in delivering a successful product.

4. **Data:** With Big Data being a dominant theme nowadays, it is trendy to include data scientists as part of the hackathon team. But before you jump onto the bandwagon, think about how you can best utilise one. Do you have existing data sets for them to work on? Or is the intent to get them to use qualitative data for storytelling? Either way is fine, but make sure that you are clear – this way no one is disappointed.

5. **Designer:** The one who will convert verbal ideas into visual concepts. Having a designer onboard

ensures that there is at least someone comfortable with sketching. Although we often stress that sketching is everyone's responsibility, the ability to produce higher-quality sketches is important as it will allow potential customers to better understand the product. Once we get to the later stages, the designer can also digitise the visuals to produce higher-fidelity prototypes.

6. **Wildcard**: This is where things get interesting. For most of the hackathons I run, I invite a startup entrepreneur to join the team. This not only brings freshness, but their hustler instincts can infectiously impart a culture change that would otherwise be hard to drive. The entrepreneur is able to participate in the full spectrum of product development activities, and stand in for any missing skillsets in the team. That said, I understand that these people can be hard to recruit. Try to look out for early-stage entrepreneurs, as they might be drawn to such events for the networks and opportunities. Also consider cash incentives or prizes to reward their participation.

The judges

Choosing the right mix of judges could have a direct effect on what gets chosen as the winning product, hence determining the success of the hackathon. Hence, I would urge all organisers to select their judges carefully.

A regular judging panel would likely include people who can actually bring the product into market. Similar to the hackers, this means representation from both the business and technology sides. However, this also means that the panel may be swayed towards ready-to-implement solutions. I would normally then balance it off with a judge who brings a macro-level vision, such as the Chief Innovation Officer or Head of Innovation. Being aware of trends, they have a vision of what the best-in-class solutions look like. We want to avoid situations where the chosen solution is a poor cousin of a market-established one, or less ambitious than projects already in the development pipeline.

Avoid having too large a judging panel, as many viewpoints might not necessarily be good. It could hamper reaching consensus and slow down decisions. Always have an odd number of judges, to avoid any deadlock when there is a tie. Three is the minimum number, while five is the optimum.

The audience

The audience will be those allowed to come and view the hackathon. We typically only invite them to view the final pitch process while the rest of the hackathon is a closed-door event. How many to invite is dependent on where the final pitch is held, but usually we expect no more than 50 people in the audience.

If the hackathon is open to the public, you might want to make the pitch a ticketed event. Audience members who bring the most value include venture capitalists (VCs), government regulators and internal staff.

VCs are welcome from an investment standpoint, as they bring funding that could propel the project forward. We've seen VCs snapping up hackathon teams and them quickly evolving into a credible startup in their own right, so do not underestimate that.

Government regulators such as the Monetary Authority of Singapore (MAS) or the Ministry of Finance would help position the hackathon organisers as a forward-thinking organisation.

Internal staff are also welcome to attend the event to generate buzz and to interest them in attending subsequent hacks. Those on the no-go list include industry competitors, who might benefit from the concepts generated.

Gearing up for the hackathon

The task force

Once the decision to host a hackathon is formalised, a task force should ideally be formed. This task force should be made up of a project manager, who will drive the entire project; the key facilitators, who will be in charge of content; and one to two project assistants. This task force is responsible for getting the following tasks done in the run-up to the hackathon.

List of attendees

To determine how many hackers to invite, first lock down the venue. For recommendations on venue selection, refer to Chapter 3, Generating High Energy. Once the venue is locked down, you roughly know how many hackers and audience you can have. Keep in mind that not everyone you invite will eventually attend. For hackers, most of the time those who RSVP will attend, and that's the same for judges. However, I can't say the same for the audience, so it is safe to over-invite by 20–30% to account for dropouts.

Sending invites

If possible, send the invites out to all proposed participants at least one month in advance. This is especially so for the judges as senior attendees tend to have very packed schedules. Use this opportunity to also send through a registration (RSVP) form to help you gather the following information:

- Full name

- Job title

- Hackathon experience – beginner (participated in zero hacks before), intermediate (three to five hacks) or advanced (more than five hacks)

- Any specific topics of interest related to the hackathon? (To allow organisers to better shape the challenge statements)

- Special needs/requests/meal requests (gluten-free, vegetarian, etc)

More information equates to better planning. Hence, make it mandatory to fill in the registration form. There are also electronic tools such as Eventbrite that could make this logistics-intensive process an easier one.

Countdown: Hackathon minus ten days

This is the best opportunity to relook the list of attendees and assess their skillsets and their level of exposure to hackathon methodology. If you have a shortage of certain skillsets, e.g. designers, there is still sufficient time for you to make it right. If your attendees are well versed in hackathon methodology, you can shorten the explanation during hackday and go straight into the activities. If it's a mixed bag or most of them are new, be more patient with explaining the rationale and process.

Recruit your table facilitators and event assistants

So far, within the task force itself you only have the one or two key facilitators. However, to run an event as interactive as a hackathon, you'll need more manpower than that. We call these people table facilitators, and they are evenly distributed around the hack room. For principles around selecting the right table facilitators, please refer to Chapter 9, Facilitation and Mentorship.

Apart from table facilitators, also remember to find helpers to run the registration table and manage the caterers. These roles could be staffed by the task force's project assistants.

Countdown: Hackathon minus three days

Keep in mind that your hackathon will live beyond the three-day span of the event. As such, a social media strategy is going to be super useful. Here's a list of things to do to help you get started:

- Do you want to create a special hashtag (e.g. #myspecialhackathon) for the hack? It helps people find out more about the event.

- Do you need a Facebook event page? If this is an internal event, there could also be a company Yammer page or intranet microsite.

- Who are the ones in charge of generating buzz on social media sites such as LinkedIn, Facebook and Twitter? Do not expect things to happen by themselves. Social media presence is often engineered.

- Do you have a team of official photographers and videographers? Tell them when the highlight events are to make sure these are captured.

Getting the right supplies

These are what I consider tools of the trade. For any successful hackathon, it is mission-critical for us to have them:

- 3M post-its. Each team should have a generous quantity of square post-its and rectangular ones.

Each person should have access to at least five pads. For a team of six, I typically provide about 30 square pads and 10–15 rectangular pads.

- Writing instruments. I personally prefer Sharpie markers but other thin markers are acceptable too. Provide one pen per attendee to allow variety.

- Prepare stickers and markers to allow attendees to write their own nametags.

- Other stationery include Blu-Tack or masking tape to allow teams to put collaterals on the wall, one roll of flipchart paper per team, scissors to cut tape, and blank A4 paper to write on.

Some other miscellaneous (but important) tasks

- Confirm your food catering order and buy lots of snacks. For guidance refer to Chapter 3.

- Email any journalists or social media influencers you know who may be interested in covering the events. These people can help create a buzz and influence public perception of your hack's success.

- A list of final attendees for security clearance to facilitate the changing of entry passes (if required).

Final email blast

This should be the last email you're sending to the attendees. At this point in time, all the logistical details should be finalised. The email should contain:

- Contact information, including a project assistant's mobile phone number so attendees can call/text if they cannot find the venue

- A high-level day plan of each day with start and end timings

- Location of the event (address and building name), exact location of entrance, directions, and map

- A reminder to bring along their ID if a change of pass is required

- A reminder to bring their laptop and charger

- Pre-reads (if any)

Countdown: Hackathon minus one day

Final event run-through

Use this opportunity to do a final check that you have the following in place:

- Each team is allocated a large table, with an additional table for the judges

- There are more than enough chairs for all the hackers, judges and audience members

- Each team to be issued an extension cord with at least five power sockets

- Wifi access for everyone

- Projectors and screen

- Two to three microphones

Print team handout

Each table should have a team handout containing the most basic information to help the team settle into the venue:

- Wifi name and password

- Event hashtag

- A high-level day plan for the next three days

Hackathon!

On the day of the hackathon itself, the task force and facilitators should arrive three hours before the start time.

- Perform a final check to make sure everything is working.

- Put up signs to guide attendees to the event venue from the first floor (don't forget signs to the washroom).

- Key facilitators to run through the slides with everyone to align expectations.

Kick-off

Upon the arrival of the 95% of the attendees or 15 minutes past the event start time (whichever happens first), run the kick-off with the following:

- Introduce the organisers. Explain the reason(s) for running the hackathon.

- Run through the logistics again – hashtags, toilets, day plans and outputs of each day.

- Encourage everyone to take photos and share on their social media.

And this is it – you're all set for action. Let the games begin, and may the best team win!

CHAPTER 2

INSIGHTS PREPARATION

FOR YOUR hackathon to take flight, you need good insights. An insights report is thus prepared before the hackathon begins, giving teams a ready launchpad for lift-off on Day 1.

Insights address three main questions: *What* is the problem we are trying to solve? *Who* are we solving it for? And *why* are we solving it? In a hackathon, qualitative insights are prized over quantitative insights. Both type of insights can contribute towards developing an amazing product, but the reason we favour qualitative insights is that they capture the "whys". Being able to know x% of customers do this and y% of customers like that is only useful to a limited extent. For us to understand the needs of our customers, we need to understand *why* the x% behave this way, and *why* the y% like that. Through further probing, you will also be able to understand the underlying motivations and emotional drivers that fuel customer satisfaction or dissatisfaction.

So what goes into an insights report? Here is a checklist to make sure you have sufficient information prepared for the hackathon teams:

Challenge statements: What are the exact problems you are getting the hackathon teams to solve? Typically each team gets issued one statement, though multiple teams can work on the same statement. The statement starts with "How might we..." and ends with a question mark. The statements can be formulated broadly at this point, allowing the teams to refine them as they embark on fieldwork (Chapter 5).

> Example: *"How might we digitise customer touch-points to increase efficiency and reduce operations cost?"*

Personas: Who are you solving the challenge for? The insights report should uncover who the target persona of the challenge statement is. It doesn't have to be very specific for now. Each team should either pick or be issued a persona that corresponds with their challenge statement. Similar to the challenge statement, the teams will be allowed to drill down deeper during fieldwork to decide on a particular persona for themselves.

> Examples: *"University students"; "mature professionals"; "young parents"*

Insight areas: A good insight area is one that sparks an Aha! moment in you. Within each area, you will find a header that summarises the area, an insight statement (more on this in

Chapter 6) and an accompanying write-up detailing the whys behind the statement. The area will also be supported by verbatim customer responses to allow the hackathon team to immerse themselves in the words of the customers. The insight areas are also relatively broad at this moment, with just enough information to get started and dig deeper into. To give an example:

> _TRACKING AND TRANSPARENCY_ [Insight area]
> _University students want to regularly check their bank balance BUT it's always a hassle to enter their pass-word for such a simple task._ [Insight statement]

Preparing the insights report

In a non-hackathon setting, this could all be done by the project team itself, but given the compressed format of a hackathon, we typically commission a third-party agency or an internal project team to prepare the report. There are three types of agencies you can choose from: market research agencies, insights agencies, and innovation consultancies.

1. Market research (MR) agencies

One of the strengths of market research agencies is that they have a strong database of respondents they can approach. If you have a short turnaround time, and need basic-level qualitative work done, MR agencies are your best bet. They also typically represent the best value for money, though this is highly dependent on how difficult it is to recruit, lead time and work required. Within this category, we have boutique examples such as Cimigo and Asia Insights, and their larger counterparts such as IPSOS, TNS and Nielsen. I've leveraged boutique MR agencies for several hackathons and so far I haven't been disappointed.

2. Insights agencies

Insights agencies provide a lot more polish, and layer more analysis and spirited copywriting over the data gathered, without going over the top with pricing. Examples of insights agencies include boutique offerings such as AGENCY (designingagency.com), and more established brand names such as FutureBrand, Quantum and Added Value. Engaging these agencies isn't cheap, but your choice hinges on how much more you value a polished product over the work of MR agencies. It might be value-for-money for some, but a deal breaker for others.

3. Innovation consultancies

At the top price tier, companies like IDEO, Frog Design, Fjord, ?What If! Innovation and Innosight will be at your disposal. The key differentiator of these consultancies is that they don't only do research, they help you think steps ahead – the exact mileage depends on which agency you are talking about. They will not only deliver a Powerpoint deck or a video, but bring artefacts, decorate the room, co-facilitate the workshop, and create an all-round immersive experience. The tech world goes by WYSIWYG (What You See Is What You Get), we in the insights world call this WYPIWYG (What You Pay Is What You Get).

How much to spend?

How much should you expect to spend on such research work? Some of the tiniest budgets I've been allocated range from S$20,000 to S$30,000. In such scenarios, I would advise recruiting an experienced freelancer. In Singapore's market, we don't have a huge pool of free-lancers, but on platforms like LinkedIn, for example, you'll be able to find ex-researchers and consultants with decades of experience. They typically offer reasonable work that is budget friendly.

When your budget goes up to the range of S$30,000–60,000, I advise going for MR or insights agencies. They will be able to conduct up to 15 in-depth, face-to-face interviews, or five to six mini focus groups of up to five respondents. I would typically also encourage them to make home visits and take photos and videos of con-versations to allow the hackathon participants to really "feel" the customers and their pain points.

The moment you have a budget above S$60,000, make an effort to contact the innovation consultancies. My experience working with them has been nothing less than spectacular. You can expect to be serviced by ex-di-rectors, heads and senior leaders of big corporations, top-tier agencies, or some really bright young talents. They always make a conscious effort to curate a team of industry natives (bankers for financial services projects) and parallel industry experts (such as in FMCGs, hospi-tality or luxury goods). Innovation consultancies are also very often at the forefront of research methodologies, and their output is always polished and professional.

Research brief

Once you've chosen what sort of agency to go with, you'll need to provide them with a written research brief. This brief is meant to delineate the boundaries of the research and to clarify intent. A typical brief looks like this:

Background: Why is this hackathon being organised?

- What is this hackathon about?

- What is the business context leading up to this hackathon and who are the key stakeholders?

- Any constraints to take note of?

Objectives: What does success look like?

- What exactly do you want to find out? For first-timers, you are probably looking at the attitudes, behaviours, pain points, problems, expectations, and opportunities of a customer segment in relation to some product.

- As follow-up to the above: Who exactly is your research segment? Make a conscious effort to get your selected agency to speak to the outliers and those who might potentially have a more professional opinion to make your research more comprehensive.

- How would this be used? The research will typically be used to kickstart ideation on Day 1 of the hackathon.

Approach: How do you want the research to be conducted?

- Do you want the agency to conduct their interviews in groups or one-on-one? One-on-one sessions are typically more useful as they give the interviewer the opportunity to ask deep questions that are difficult to get to in a group setting. They also prevent groupthink, where a loud respondent leads the entire conversation and others follow suit, skewing your data.

- Do you want to explore online research? Online groups, on Facebook, WhatsApp or any other social media or chat platform, can be interesting as they provide a channel for "just in time" engagement. Imagine if you want to find out your respondent's experience queuing for an ATM. Instead of asking them to recall, you'll get a much better understanding from going out there and experiencing it live and getting real-time feedback.

- Are you open to exploring other types of research? If you're engaging a cutting-edge consultancy for this work, leave this portion open and allow them to impress you with what they may come up with!

Everything else: What other points should the agency take note of?

- What type of reporting format do you want? Powerpoint slides are good, but always also ask for posters, illustrations and summary of findings on A1/A0-size sheets to put up on the walls.

- Do you want the agency to be present at the hackathon itself? Certainly, good external speakers can bring freshness and an additional dimension to the hackathon. But let's be honest, not all good researchers are good presenters. If your agency partner is capable of producing the work, but seems like a dull presenter, consider doing it yourself. It adds to your credibility as facilitator too.

- What is the timeline you are working with? Give your agency partner at least three weeks' turnaround time. If you're really short of time (e.g. one week), go for an MR agency. Other types of agencies and consultancies typically outsource the recruitment of respondents to MR agencies anyway, you can buy yourself some time by going to the source.

- What is your budget estimate? If you have plenty of time, tell your shortlisted agencies that you have no fixed budget in mind and see what interesting ideas they come back with. I tend to work with really tight timelines, so I usually tell the agencies how much I have upfront. If they are keen, great, otherwise I can immediately look for someone else.

- Do you have any existing research dataset that you would like to incorporate as the starting point of this research? For now, all you have to do is to flag that there is existing data available. Don't send the actual data to the chosen agency until after the contract of engagement and Non-Disclosure Agreement have been signed.

Finally, once you have selected your agency, nailed down the approach, boundaries and timelines, you can breathe slightly easier. Try to be there in person during research, as your physical presence is going to highlight the importance of the research work. You can also observe if the research is on track or off track early, so that you will not be in for a rude shock at the very end.

What if you have no budget?

This is a very valid question to ask as it is commonly faced by many new hackathon organisers. With no successful track record to show, and scant regard for the hackathon methodology by the upper echelons, getting a substantial budget for research seems almost impossible.

To circumvent this situation, I typically pull together an internal cross-functional research team to run a pre-hack sprint to help us gather insights. Leverage the hackathon tools we use in the subsequent chapters (Chapters 4,5 and 6). The team first draws up a stakeholder map to define who our customers and their wider network of connections are. Then we choose a list of 20 respondents to interview before consolidating what we find into insights. The insights and personas identified would make up the research which we bring into the hackathon itself.

Also, remember to spend some effort on desk research. Plough through the internet for research done by management consultancies (e.g. McKinsey, Bain, BCG, PwC) to supplement what you might have. Megatrend infographics are also useful, to supplement the research coming out of the pre-hack sprint. Remember to set aside at least a month of lead time for the internal team. Most of them won't be insights professionals, and may need more time to produce good outputs than their professional counterparts.

Putting it all together

The entire research process – whether you're outsourcing the insights preparation or doing it in-house – should crystallize into the challenge statements, personas and insight areas that I mentioned at the start of this chapter. These will address the three questions – what we want to solve, who we are solving it for, and why we want to solve it.

An example from a recent hackathon I ran looks like this:

> *"How might we address the evolving needs of our millennial customers by offering a credit product that would grow along with them?"*

This statement recognizes the who (millennials); the what (customer needs in this segment change rapidly as millennials transit from being undergraduates to working adults to young parents all within the short span of a decade); and the why (business objective of up-selling our credit products).

Such insights build up an immersive experience for the hackathon participants. But how many insights do you need? I am tempted to say the more the merrier of course! However, taking a realistic point of view, we say enough when we have achieved a working-level understanding of what, who and why. In practical terms, that means having spoken to real customers (not one or two, but a lot of them), landed on four to five tangible insights and identified several opportunities to work on. This should also culminate in three to four persona posters – the aggregation of all those you've spoken to – to really understand how a "typical" customer will look, feel and behave.

Armed with strong insights, we can now move into the next phase of the hackathon.

CHAPTER 3

GENERATING HIGH ENERGY

HACKATHONS ARE best known for animated exchanges between immensely talented participants. This does not happen by chance. In this chapter, I will provide tips around how to ensure high energy in the room, and also give you a list of energisers that can help you pull your participants out of a slump.

Right number of attendees + right room = fantastic hackathon

A key factor in creating a great hackathon atmosphere is selecting the right room. Seemingly easy, this is crucial for new hackathon organisers to get right, as the wrong room can be a drag on subsequent activities regardless of how well-planned they might be.

A good hackathon room...

As a rule of thumb, I generally plan for hackathons with 30–40 attendees in mind. If each team has six members, this gives us five to six teams. This is the golden ratio, in my opinion. Any larger and you risk losing control of the room; any smaller and it's really hard to get the momentum going. Some of the best hackathons I've conducted have been those with around 40 attendees.

From a judging standpoint, seven teams of ten minutes' presentation each (five minutes' pitch with three to five minutes of Q&A) would take slightly over an hour. Any longer might make it hard for the judges to sit through the entire event.

If I have about 40 participants, I typically ask for a room that's 20 x 20 meters in dimension, with floor-to-ceiling windows

... sets you up for success!

on at least one side of the room. This ensures lots of natural daylight, which has been shown to help people think more creatively and uplift their mood.

Make sure that the room has a generous number of power sockets as each team will need to have at least one near them. Extension cords are also a must – all of us now carry several devices with us and require additional power over the course of the day.

The furniture in the room is another important factor to consider. Avoid any room with a big boardroom table. Such tables are normally fixed to the floor. We want flexible furniture that can be reconfigured whenever necessary.

DBS's innovation lab, DBS Asia X (DAX), is designed with all the above criteria in mind. No fixed furniture, floor-to-ceiling windows on two sides, bright lighting, speakers for music wired throughout the space, and noise-absorbent carpet to finish off an amazing innovation space, enough said.

Creating an all-time high

Even with the perfect room, a high-energy hackathon is not a given. I have been to hackathons where participants were bored or even completely uninterested in the work. Such responses are typically due to two reasons: the participants could have been forced by their superiors to attend the event; or the tasks given to them were too overwhelming and they switched off after a while. The research of distinguished psychologist Mihaly Csikszentmihalyi is worth bearing in mind here – participants enter their most optimal state, the peak of their creative abilities, only when the task is not too mundane or too stressful.

How then can we ensure that despite the daunting challenges, participants maintain a healthy amount of interest and are driven to achieve their best? Here are several ways:

Hackers need their coffee

From my experience, more than 90% of hackathon attendees tend to be serious coffee addicts. This seems to be very prevalent among creative types! Make an effort to rent a capsule espresso machine or get tumblers of black coffee from

Starbucks. If budget permits, get a barista in to make fresh coffee. It is definitely a worthwhile investment to make for the ideas that come out of the caffeinated minds.

Feed them well

Couple the coffee with a generous amount of food (either individually packed bentos or buffet-style) during lunch and afternoon tea breaks, to make the hackathon experience complete. If possible, go easy on the carbs – they only make the attendees sleepy without much benefits.

Bring on the sugar rush

Place lots of chocolates, candy and snacks on every table, for whenever someone feel a little lethargic. Get snacks that are individually wrapped, e.g. Snickers bars – this results in less wastage, higher take-up, and a cleaner hackathon room.

Leave the beer tap running

In the evenings, free-flow beer – on tap or in bottles – allows people to unwind, bond, or simply have a good drink before they soldier on. Hackathons are high-stress events, so knowing when to pile on the pressure and when to unwind allows them to have an enjoyable experience. This special perk will also draw younger programmers and designers, and they are integral to any hackathon!

Energisers

Energisers are excellent short activities for generating high energy during a hackathon. Here I share three of the most commonly used ones, and the intention behind each of them.

Energiser 1: No-look portrait

No-look portrait is a fantastic tool to get the day started and to break the ice. You can also use this opportunity to gauge how familiar the attendees are with the hackathon methodology and adjust your approach accordingly.

1. Start by pairing up all the participants.
2. Hand each participant a sheet of A5 paper and a Sharpie marker.
3. Everyone now has 30 seconds to draw the face of their partner. However, they must do so without looking down at what they are drawing. Not even a quick glance is allowed! (It's part of the fun for the drawings to go wildly off course.)
4. After the 30 seconds, the participants swap drawings with their partners, so that they're now holding on to the "portraits" of themselves.
5. Everyone writes his/her name under their "portrait".
6. Ask everyone in the room, "On a scale of 1 to 10, how familiar are you with hackathons?"
7. Within teams, the participants now take turns to introduce themselves and talk about how familiar they are with hackathons. This activity should be supervised by the table facilitators.
8. Once done, put everyone's portrait up on the walls – this helps to personalise the room and foster a sense of belonging to the space.

Energiser 2: Animal name race

This activity fosters teamwork and improves communication. It comes in handy when teams are facing issues agreeing on a certain point of view, by helping them gain alignment. Or simply use it to pull them out of post-lunch slumps.

1. This is a team-based activity. Each team prepares by writing the 26 letters of the alphabet on their flipchart. We typically use a two-column format, with 13 letters in each column.

2. Get each team to line up in front of their flipchart in single file. The first person is handed a Sharpie marker.

3. Now explain that each person will have to fill in the name of an animal that corresponds with each letter of the alphabet. They will take turns to fill in the names one by one, in sequence. No skipping or double-filling allowed. They are not allowed to communicate with each other or check their mobile phones while playing the game. If the person answering is stuck, his/her teammates can only help by acting out that particular animal.

4. Shout "Go!" and get the teams to start. The fastest team to complete all 26 letters with zero mistakes wins.

5. Tip: For the trickier letters such as U, V and X, ask the teams to use their creativity. And if everyone gets it wrong, at least the fastest one wins!

Answers: Ant, Bear, Cat, Deer, Elephant, Fish, Goat, Horse, Iguana, Jaguar, Kangaroo, Leopard, Monkey, Nightingale, Octopus, Pig, Quail, Rabbit, Sheep, Tiger, Uguisu, Vulture, Wolf, X-ray tetra, Yak, Zebra

Energiser 3: Twenty post-its

This activity is a great warm-up for brainstorming.

1. Each team takes 20 post-its and sticks them on the team's table in a 5 x 4 grid.
2. Explain that for the next three minutes, the teams will have to fill in each post-it with a drawing of a different square/rectangular object. For example, if the post-it represents a lunch box, the team should draw out how the lunch box looks in the post-it given.
3. Allow them to express their creativity or link the post-its up to create bigger objects if required.
4. The winner is judged on speed *and* diversity of objects. (I once had a team who drew different mahjong tiles on each of the post-its. Although they were the fastest to finish, they didn't win because all the objects were similar. Another team who took a longer time but had all different items won.)

Bonus Energiser: Human rock paper scissors

A great way to re-inject some energy back into the attendees. Use this opportunity to step out of the usual space for a change of environment.

1. Everyone looks for a partner to play rock paper scissors with.
2. The loser follows behind the winner as supporter and cheers for the winner.
3. The winner then looks for another attendee to play against. The loser, together with any existing supporters, joins in the line of the winner. Repeat this again until two long lines of supporters emerge.
4. The final two face off to decide the grand champion!

CHAPTER 4

HUMAN-CENTRED DESIGN I: PRE-FIELDWORK

THE SCARIEST PART of a hackathon starts when participants are locked in the hackathon room and feel the sudden pressure to "innovate" in a short time. Very often, this is when they start to regret their very decision to take part! But fret not. From this chapter onwards, we will shift gears, going from organiser to participant mode, to get you up to speed on a methodology that can turn anyone who enters the hackathon room into an innovator, and can generate solutions that answer real human needs, hopes and aspirations.

Human-Centred Design (HCD) is a highly researched and repeatable methodology that really anyone can put into use. I especially mean those who lament that they have no time, those who cite a hundred and one reasons like business constraints, budget, previous failures, etc., and those who feel that they have left their creativity behind in their childhood.

For all who feel like they are stuck, HCD can rekindle the spark.

The starting point of HCD is that customers are humans, not robots. To fully understand them, we have to address their higher-order needs, tracing out patterns of human behaviour that would be neglected if we only looked at their basic needs. To help quantify the different types of needs your customers have, we typically approach it from three angles: functional, emotional and social needs.

- **Functional needs** are utilitarian – what customers need simply to get their job done. For example, if you are sleepy and want coffee, you go to the nearest coffee joint to get it. Functionally your need is satisfied. However, if the service staff are rude or the wait is too long, you will leave with coffee in hand but still feel emotionally dissatisfied.

- To address your **emotional needs**, the coffee joint might send all their staff for service training and relook their workflow to deliver the coffee in the quickest way possible.

- **Social needs** are how you want to be perceived when entering the coffee joint and holding the cup of coffee afterwards. In the past, Starbucks might be the default "cool" coffee brand, but nowadays those who wish to be perceived as "in-the-know" might choose to buy a hand-dripped brew from a specialty cafe that costs twice as much as an americano from Starbucks.

To tackle these needs, which are often hidden to customers themselves, I will share in Chapters 4, 5, and 6 the HCD tools that let you peer beneath the surface. The 12 steps of this process, which will span across these three chapters, are:

Step 1	Deciphering the challenge statement
Step 2	Persona hypothesis
Step 3	User ecosystem
Step 4	Research planning
Step 5	Method of engagement
Step 6	Discussion guide
Step 7	Conducting interviews
Step 8	Storytelling and clustering
Step 9	Writing an insight
Step 10	Setting boundary questions
Step 11	Brainstorming
Step 12	Conceptualisation

Three HCD mindsets to live by

Be a team player

Do not embark on the HCD process alone. Having partners and team members allows you to learn from each other. HCD values having multiple perspectives, which is only possible when you are challenged to step out of your own shoes. If you come to a consensus, this gives you stronger validation; but if you do not, take time to understand why.

Be positive-minded

Have faith that HCD can solve your problem no matter how big or small it is. The HCD process is a highly researched and field-tested methodology that delivers. If you are lost during the process, let your positivity guide you and soldier on! Ensure that you do not dismiss other people's points-of-view; instead choose to build on them. If you're saying "No... but" too often (e.g. "No, we've tried that before, but our bosses didn't like it"), it's time to start saying "Yes... and" (e.g. "Yes, let's try that again, and we can enhance it by...").

Be audacious

Do not be afraid to make mistakes, or to sound "dumb". Learn to question and challenge. Do not take the status quo at face value; instead always challenge norms and beliefs. This will lead you to rethink the many fundamental assumptions that we all make on a daily basis.

Step 1. Deciphering the challenge statement

The hackathon process usually starts off with challenge statements. Each team will either be issued one or be given a chance to choose their ideal challenge statement. Once you have a statement in hand, stick it at the top of the flipchart or whiteboard given to the team. This will serve as the guiding principle that the team will work towards over the next three days.

Typical challenge statements look like this:

A. *"How might we redesign our current credit card offering to better suit the needs of millennials?"*

B. *"How might we digitise the branch experience so that we can provide a 100% self-served experience?"*

C. *"How might we make Singapore a cashless society?"*

The three statements are similar in a few ways. They all start with "How might we" and end with a question mark. This is to frame the statement as a question, allowing participants to jumpstart the process and go straight into the ideation and brainstorming process.

Yet they are also different. Statement A looks at designing a *product* for a particular segment; statement B focuses on the designing of a *digital experience*; while statement C is a more macro challenge of designing for an *ideal state*. All three are valid, meaty challenges that could lead to exciting new products and services for the organisation hosting the hackathon.

When you receive the challenge statement, read it aloud. I typically do this thrice, so that I internalise it. Next try to read for context. What are the constraints and boundaries that you have to work with?

For statement A, you're designing for millennials – this is useful data but you have to keep in mind that millennials are people who were born any time between the early 1980s and the early 2000s (by the broadest definition). There can be a huge disparity between the two ends of the age spectrum. This statement also prescribes the need for the product to be a credit card – which can be limiting because it could be that at the end of our discussion we might not want to design a credit card but something related or similar.

For statement B, the 100% self-served experience is a Big Hairy Audacious Goal (BHAG) that the host organisation has set out to achieve. Such goals are a commonplace in the banking world right now – therefore slightly easier as you can then Google and gain some inspiration off the internet.

For statement C, this is typically seen in hackathons run by government departments or big incumbents. There are no explicit constraints given, which gives the participants almost the right for blue-sky thinking. (Note that this lack of constraints can mean disaster sometimes, so please understand the context around the ideal state described.)

The next step is to plough through all the datapoints, research documents, and insights reports given, to make sure you get the full context. At this point, the facilitators should have already shared some background around the challenges or topics of the day – look back at your notes and align all your team members towards a common understanding.

Step 2. Persona hypothesis

The persona hypothesis is where we start to bring the *human* into the HCD process. It is termed "hypothesis" as this is the first instance where we start to collaboratively brainstorm who the end customer should be. This is also a strong reminder that whatever we come up with at this stage is a hypothesis and not the absolute truth.

The first question to ask is: What does our typical customer look like? Draw a quick sketch in the box on the top left hand corner of the persona hypothesis template. You don't have to be an artist for this exercise: the idea is simply to put a face to the name, to constantly remind yourself that you are solving for a real customer.

Next, fill in his/her demographic data – age, gender and job (remember we're gunning for the average and not one precise individual). We then proceed to give our persona a name. This is to make it feel like you're solving for a real person rather than just going through an academic exercise.

Persona

Name

Hui min

Age

24

Job

Undergrad

Key Traits/Behaviours

1. Wants to experience the world on a shoestring budget
2. Values new experiences over repeat destinations
3. Low brand loyalty, and easily swayed by promotions
4. Works part-time to fund travels and activities outside of school.

Blockers

1. Peer pressure to spend on premium alternatives
2. Wants in life, such as branded handbags.

Leveraging the basic demographic data we've captured so far, we'll jump into the deeper conversations. Discuss among your team: What are the key traits/behaviours of our typical customers? Some examples could be:

- *"He is a millennial and an active user of cards with more than 30 transactions a month."*

- *"She works for a shop nearby and has to go to the branch every day to deposit her daily earnings."*

- *"She visits the hawker centre on a daily basis and has to always remember her spare change."*

Capture as many of these traits as possible, as they will form the discussion points of your conversations with your customers subsequently.

The next field is blockers. As a team, brainstorm potential pointers that have stopped your typical customers from getting the best experience of their life. Remember, these are all assumptions waiting to be verified. Some responses in this field might be:

- *"Limited credit card promotions"*

- *"Robots cannot deliver customised services"*

- *"Lack of infrastructure"*

Land each of the discussion points on a post-it note.

Do note that there may be instances where there are two or more personas for the particular challenge statement. That is perfectly normal, especially when you're given something as broad as the earlier statement C, which concerns changing the behaviour of an entire country. In such situations, first land the basic demographic data of all the possible customer types, then proceed to zoom in to the full persona template for one or two whom you feel will be *early adopters* of the product or service that you're trying to design. These early adopters are the ones whom you'll have the biggest impact and greatest success with.

Step 3. User ecosystem

Once we've identified the persona of our customers, we can proceed to look into the complex network of relationships that play a part in the particular transaction or experience that we're trying to create.

Put the persona you've defined in the middle of the user ecosystem template. Now discuss as a team: Who has the ability to influence our targeted customer's purchase decision or experience?

Let's consider the user ecosystem for this persona:

> *He is a millennial and an active user of cards with more than 30 transactions a month.*

First up, can we safely assume that his decisions are influenced by his peers? Certainly. Draw a line out from the user and write down "Friends". Who then influences his friends? Famous bloggers? Check. Draw a line out from "Friends" and write down "Bloggers" (bonus points if you can name one or two of these bloggers).

Remember, the more detail you have, the more complete your ecosystem is. Who influences these bloggers then? Merchants? Since many of these bloggers' posts are sponsored, it's highly likely that merchants have a big part to play in the process. Draw a line out to "Merchants". How about celebrities? Many of these bloggers are followers of American and British artistes; land these as well. Once we get to the third or fourth degree, it's sufficiently detailed.

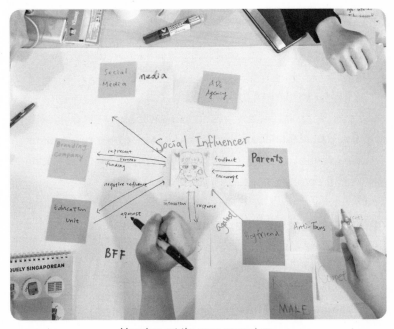

Mapping out the user ecosystem

Let's try another typical relationship that sways millennials. How about their boy/girlfriend? Who influences their partners? Bloggers? Draw a line between "Partner" with "Blogger" and we have what is called a *triangulated relationship*. Apart from bloggers, could their parents also be a major source of influence? Sure, land that. Who influences their parents? Traditional media (television, radio, newspapers) is a possibility; their employers (if they're still working) and their siblings are all potential influences too.

At this point you must be wondering, how does the radio influence our persona's purchase decisions? Look at it this way, if our persona actively seeks out his/her partner's advice when applying for a credit card, and his/her partner's perception on money is shaped by their parents who then got their information from the radio – *you know where to park your marketing budget now!*

Step 4. Research planning

Once you've landed on your target persona, and mapped out who influences their decisions, it's time to step out of the hackathon room to validate your assumptions. Before doing so, however, you'll need to come up with a concrete research plan. A typical research plan includes who you want to speak to, how you wish to approach them, and which category each respondent belongs to.

Within the research plan itself, there are three fields. Who, Why and When:

Research Plan

Who	Why	When

- **Who** is the person you're trying to engage? You'll be looking to engage people you identified in your persona hypothesis and user ecosystem. A generic description like "teacher" will not make the cut. Write down the name of the teacher, or even better, his/her contact information so that we know that this is a real person you could approach. Remember, this is who we actually intend to speak to and not a dream list, hence selecting your primary school teacher whom you haven't contacted in 15 years (and have no way of reaching) probably won't work.

- **Why** is very important as this allows anyone in the team to pick up the research plan and understand the principle behind speaking to this individual and how to structure the conversation.

- **When** would require you to do some high-level planning. Beyond listing down a potential date and time to reach out to individual respondents, think about who you want to interview first and always remember that you can further segment the group to ensure that you get the most work done in the least time possible. Remember, in a three-day hackathon, you don't have a lot of time. Researchers from the Nielsen Norman Group suggest that five is typically the optimum number to capture the bulk of the learning. We concur with their findings and recommend you speak to five to seven people from your user ecosystem.

Have you landed several personas, drawn up the ecosystems of your potential customers, and hatched a plan to speak to them? If the answer is yes, you are now ready to step out of the hackathon room and into the field! At this point, if you are still unsure about what you should actually do with these people you have arranged to meet, that's absolutely natural. The next chapter will shed light on the methods of engagement to ensure each interaction is fruitful, productive and efficient.

CHAPTER 5

HUMAN-CENTRED DESIGN II: FIELDWORK

IN THE PREVIOUS chapter, we learnt the tools and methods for you to better understand your customers (through the persona hypothesis), their life and network (via user ecosystem mapping), and made a plan to engage them (via research planning). The next step is to actually step out of the hackathon room and engage with your potential customers, through a process called fieldwork.

In a typical three-day hackathon, fieldwork takes up the second half of Day 1. In this chapter, we will talk about the art and science of fieldwork – from methods of engagement, to knowing what questions to ask, to how to collate the information learnt into something meaningful.

Step 5. Method of engagement

One aspect where HCD shines as compared to the regular (or Business-As-Usual/BAU) way of solving problems, is the way we engage the customers. In HCD, we advocate a mixture of three different engagement methods, namely *Be them*, *With them* and *About them*. These methods allow us to gain deeper insights as compared to the usual questionnaires or surveys that businesses conduct.

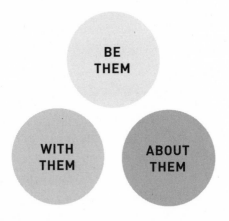

- **Method 1: Be them**, and I really mean *be* your respondent. If your challenge is about credit card application, apply for one now and understand how that feels. If your challenge is about branch experience, step into a branch now to under-stand how branch visitors feel. If it is about going cashless, leave your cash behind and go out for a meal. These actions will give you first-hand expe-rience of the challenge you're trying to resolve and help engender empathy for the personas whom you're solving the challenge for.

- **Method 2: With them** is observation. See how people react on the ground when going through the transaction or experience. You get to see, feel, experience the pain and problems your respondents encounter and ask questions to help you gain a deeper understanding of the particular interaction.

- **Method 3: About them** refers to in-depth conversations you have with your customers (ideally after the *Be them* and *With them* segments) to clear any doubts and uncover the whys behind what you see. These conversations form the foundation of the insights and give you the opportunity to validate any assumptions or clarify any misconceptions you might have.

Using a mixture of these methods will allow us to understand what the customers say versus what they actually do. As Henry Ford is believed to have once said: "If I had asked people what they wanted, they would have said faster horses." This quote exemplifies the pitfalls of sticking to one method of engagement. Never take what the customer says at face value. Hackathon participants should be familiar with all three methods of engagement and be ready to use them whenever necessary to better understand the life of the target persona.

Outliers and extremes
In the world of innovation, we often aspire towards disruptive or transformative innovation. As a seasoned innovator

myself, I can assure you that speaking to the usual suspects is rarely sufficient to get you there. Speaking to your usual customers will only allow you to validate what you already

Why not surveys?

Through my experiences working in and out of the banking sector, I have realised that surveys are the default way to collect data. However, due to the predominant use of yes/no questions, surveys do not give us sufficient context around why customers choose a particular option. They leave little room for HCD teams to dig for insights. The why behind respondents' particular likes and dislikes holds far more value than the response itself, which explains why we prefer to be out in the field and not behind computers collecting data.

Secondly, there is often a poor choice of timing for conducting these surveys. I often see businesses adopting two approaches, either immediately after an engagement, by asking people for voluntary feedback, or setting up a kiosk and approaching people who are rushing from location to location. There is little impetus for those who have enjoyed good service to stay on the line to give feedback, whereas those who volunteer to be surveyed are probably hopping mad from the poor service they received, leading to skewed data sets. The other method of intercepting commuters in a rush leads to respondents who reluctantly accept the request, or are probably thinking about where they should be heading next, such that they refrain from giving meatier responses.

know. It brings you towards incremental innovation – small steps in the right direction.

But when you join a hackathon, you're there to win. Therefore, I recommend speaking to customers with an *extreme* relationship with the service or product you're trying to design.

For example, in the world of credit card application, on the one hand you have people who have 25 active cards. On the other end of the spectrum, you have middle-aged housewives who are highly sceptical of cards and plan their life exclusively around the use of cash. These people are your outliers. If you manage to address their needs which deviate so much from the norm, you are well on your way to creating earth-shattering impact.

Step 6. Discussion guide

For a typical three-day hackathon, I normally recommend that the teams prepare a list of ten questions for engaging their respondents. The questions should be divided into two categories – broad, and deep:

- **Broad:** List down five questions that will help you establish a rapport with and frame the context for your respondent. Start by asking them to introduce themselves. Identify the "me too" moments within the introduction to find commonalities between both of you, be it an interest, a place you travelled to, or an area you lived in. Once you've warmed up the conversation, go into the broad themes you're trying to address. What is the most recent credit card you applied for? What attracted you to apply for that card? When was the last time you came over to the branch? What was that for? These are all typical questions to help us set the stage for the subsequent conversation.

- **Deep:** Start by validating the blockers you've identified during the formation of the persona. What stopped you from getting one of these cards? Can you describe the best experience you had so far? What else do you think we can do to make your experience a better one? What do you think about a competitor's solution? Would you use it? These are all valid questions that hackathon participants could ask their respondents.

However, make sure that you do not follow the guide blindly. Whenever you hear a response that is interesting, please go with it and ask as many whys as possible. The strength of a great interviewer is his/her ability to sniff out the interesting points mentioned by the respondent and follow these leads without being constrained by the original interview script.

Step 7. Conducting interviews

With your discussion guide and research plan in place, you're now ready to embark on the interviewing process. Here are some top tips for this stage of work:

The interview is a multi-sensory experience

Remember to open your eyes, observe how your respondents talk about certain topics. Sometimes, what you see is a lot more valuable than what you hear. When they are talking about the number of credit cards they have, or how mobile-savvy they are, ask them to show you, or ask for a demo on the spot. The less preparation they do, the more accurate it gets. Ask them to relate their emotions or preference on a color palette (Which color do you think represents millennials? Why?) or using texture (Which texture feels more luxurious?). This might not give you a direct datapoint but will be very useful as you work towards your first minimum viable product (MVP) in the later stages of the hackathon.

Scribble first and interpret later

The most ideal interview unit is a team of two, where one focuses on asking questions, and the other on recording everything heard into a notebook. At this stage, no interpretation is required; the recorder just has to write everything down verbatim. The interviewer's job is to practise active listening so that he/she can ask follow-up questions to uncover the *why* behind the customer's statements.

Try not to go as a team of three as can be quite intimidating for the respondent. If you do have three, though, the third person should focus on taking photos – of the interview, the environment, the interactions, and any data that the recorder is unable to capture.

Probe your way to an effective interview

In an article I wrote for *Huffington Post*, I outlined five effective probes that skilful innovation practitioners use:

1. **The Mirror**, where you repeat back what you've just heard and ask, what's next?

2. **The Why**, where the interviewer asks why whenever he/she stumbles on an interesting point – remember, it's never about asking *all* the questions on your discussion guide. If your gut feeling tells you to pursue a particular line of inquiry, chances are you should. When asking why, try not to ask it more than five times as that's where it starts to feel irritating.

3. **The Affirmative**, where you make sounds of positive acknowledgement whenever the respondent makes a comment.

4. **The Silence** is used by skilful practitioners to give respondents time to think and reflect, instead of filling in all the discussion time with a non-stop sequence of questions.

5. **The Hook** is used to tease information out of closed-up respondents. When you mention to

them what other people said in previous interviews, they will usually feel more comfortable
sharing their opinions.

When and where to conduct these interviews
The one big tip I give to anyone seeking to conduct sponta-
neous interviews is to look for people who are stuck in a particular scenario for an extended period of time. This includes
those who are there voluntarily and have some time on hand.
Examples of these situations include smokers at various
smoking points, people queuing for products/services and
those who are reading in cafes. If you read the situation right,
they will very often be happy to spare 15 minutes or more to
go through the interview with you.

Step 8. Storytelling and clustering

After getting the fieldwork done, we need a systematic way
to help everyone get onto the same page. This is especially
important if you have been operating as sub-groups where
not everyone is up to date on each other's findings.

To get past that, we get into the storytelling mode immediately after fieldwork. But why storytelling? The key reason is
that everyone loves a good story. And it forces you to relook

Notes   Clues   Themes   Insights   How might we?   Ideas

Storytelling and clustering to get everyone on the same page

the messy **notes** you captured during the interview process and clean them up into what we call **clues**. Clues are what you heard, saw or experienced, typically expressed verbatim, with no interpretation added. Each clue is written on square post-its, giving you the flexibility to move it around when you move into clustering.

Example of a good clue:

"I want to start saving for the future of my children as tertiary education is getting more expensive year on year." – Alice, housewife, mother of two (aged 7 and 9)

Example of a bad clue:

"Tertiary education is expensive."
(There is no context to this statement, leaving us unsure of who said it and why he/she said so.)

For each of the 30-minute interviews you have conducted, try to come up with at least 20 clues that will be pieced together as part of the persona's story.

Clustering the clues around themes

Now let's revisit the persona hypothesis we created in the previous chapter. Invite someone to kickstart the sharing process. Say:

> "This is X (name of interviewee) for persona Y (the persona you are referencing)."

Start by sharing some basic demographic details of your respondent. What does X do? How old is X? Where did you meet X? How did you know X?

Next, share the single most inspiring datapoint you've captured about X – remember that a story is more than just reciting facts. Cut to the struggle of your respondent. Make sure it is completely verbatim. Stick the post-it under the assumed persona Y.

Now, invite others to share. Call out:

> "Do you have anything similar?"

This is clustering, leading us to themes. Follow up with, "How is this similar? Does this also apply to other personas?" Start shifting the post-it notes around, and end the conversation

How fieldwork allowed Ford to learn that drivers judge the speed of a car by its look and feel?

In the late 1990s, Ford received complaints from customers that the latest Mustang model seemed weaker than previous versions. It disturbed the engineers because the engine horsepower was in fact higher than previous generations. Surveys did not help them resolve this mystery.

What helped them get answers was when Ford hired a consulting company to engage their customers using the "With them" approach. By riding along with the new Mustang owners, observing and interviewing as they drove, the seasoned ethnographers uncovered a hidden insight: a car's power was a constructed image within customers' minds. They learnt that drivers made their decisions on whether a car looked like a fast car based on its exterior modelling, how "powerful" the engine sounded and how much vibration they felt through the steering wheel.

This resulted in a complete overhaul of the Mustang design. The new model, as described by Richard Hutting, Ford California's Design Chief, "has that sense of motion even when it is standing still. It captures your eyes from 50 feet away and is instantly recognised as an Mustang."

with a larger post-it (such as the 8" x 6" ones) at the top of the pile highlighting what this theme is.

If the theme identified is applicable for other persona, replicate the theme post-it for the other persona. Remember, personas are living documents. We use the word "hypothesis" for a reason. If at any point, you want to edit some of assumptions you or your teammates wrote earlier, feel free to do so.

Now move on to another clue. What is one of the most surprising things you heard your respondent say? Run through the same procedure of inviting your teammates to build on what you have.

Next, what are the pain points, barriers and opportunities you've identified? Run through all of them. Towards the end you should have exhausted all your post-it notes. Another teammate takes over from here and follows the same sequence to exhaust his/her post-it notes.

Once everyone is done with this exercise, your team will have arrived at an updated persona hypothesis and lots of different clues being landed and sorted into theme clusters.

CHAPTER 6

HUMAN-CENTRED DESIGN III: IDEATION

ONCE WE HAVE clustered our clues into various themes, we are one step away from landing insights from the fieldwork conducted. These insights supplement those provided by the agencies (see Chapter 2), and help teams gain an in-depth understanding of their persona of choice.

To recap, we started our HCD journey by defining our persona, before going out there and speaking to them, then assembling our clues and themes. Now we need to up the ante and really get behind what all these actually mean.

"Insight" is one of the most overused and misunderstood words in the English language. Insights are neither data-points, nor facts nor summaries. We only consider them insights when they offer fresh perspective into understanding the customer, allowing us to move from *what* to *why*. This is one of the most important turning points in the hackathon journey as we shift gears to go into solutioning mode once we land on some solid insights.

Step 9. Writing an insight

We can think of an insight as a dilemma. This is a statement that articulates two opposing truths, presenting us with a problem waiting to be solved. Let me give an example:

> *"Millennials in Singapore understand the importance of savings **but** overspend their pay cheque every month."*

In this particular example, we see that two truths that we discovered during the research process have been brought together by the word "but", giving a clear indication of the problem to be solved. A good insight should be a revelation, allowing us to see a particular issue from a different angle, one that we might otherwise miss without such a juxtaposition.

In their purest form, then, insights can be expressed using this framework:

       Truth A   but   *Truth B*   .

Note that there are several qualifiers as to how we teach and use this in hackathons.

- This is just one of the many ways to write insights, and the one favoured by DBS Innovation Group as the default hackathon insight framework.

- Truth A and Truth B can be drawn from the clues and themes identified. They can also be quantitative datapoints such as "70% of our customers would immediately call our call centre if they lost their credit card".

- To help the insight statement flow linguistically, you can also choose to use the words "yet" or "however" in place of "but".

Formulating insights is often the hardest skill to teach, but if done well yields the greatest impact for your hackathon team. Some other reminders to keep in mind:

- **The greater the tension, the meatier the challenge**. There might be several contrasting statements you can make out of the conversations you had. But this is not just about seeking contrast. We want contradictions, a fresh perspective, one that hasn't been seen or thought of before.

- **Three is a good number.** For a typical hackathon, seek three good insights. This is the bare minimum we need to produce two to three good concepts subsequently. Make sure that the insights do not overlap with each other and are unique.

- **Insights are not data, facts or ideas.** Many first-time hackathon participants often fall into the trap of positioning data (such as clues), facts (commonly understood truths without having to do any fieldwork), or ideas/solutions as insights. In the first instance they may appear intuitively correct, but if you substitute true insights with any of these, you may have difficulty generating solutions that really target the issue.

- **Use simple language.** If your insights cannot be understood by your teammates, there may be too many technicalities in there. Try to rewrite your complex insights into simpler sentences, so that they are understandable by everyone. Follow Albert Einstein's advice: "Everything should be as simple as possible, but not simpler."

Step 10. Setting boundary questions

To get from raw insights to actionable business ideas, we first need to flip the insights into "How might we...?" questions. This process will test whether we truly understand the insights and can re-express them for the larger hackathon team.

The questions also set up a *boundary* for your subsequent ideation. If they are too broad you may land on super generic solutions; if too narrow, you will not move the needle (and not win the hackathon).

For example, if your insight is "Millennials are not apply- ing for credit cards, which they find outdated, but they still require unsecured loans and credit facilities as they bring financial flexibility", you might potentially land on the bound- ary question of "How might we design a more millennial-rel- evant credit facility that would suit their lifestyle and needs?" By framing your question this way, you've set the boundary of the ideation around "credit facility", hence the solution would have to be a variant of "unsecured loan" in one way or another. The notion of "millennial-relevant" also helps you frame your target audience, using what the insight statement provided.

An example of a narrower boundary question would be "How might we make millennials apply for more credit cards?" In this instance, the credit card form factor has already been decided, leaving very little room for the hackathon team to navigate and express their creativity. This is also written from the organisational standpoint, as selling more credit cards to millennials sounds more like a KPI than what a customer would actually desire. Rethink this and start from the cus- tomer's perspective.

An example of a broader boundary question would be "How might we redesign payments for millennials?" While broad, the question lacks perspective. Hence, ideas could go anywhere from barter trade as a payment method, to biometric-linked payment chips embedded in your thumb as a payment method. Unless this is the exact intent, avoid going complete "blue sky" as it would mean that you will have a more difficult time tying it back to the business impact in the subsequent phases.

As mentioned, your question should be sufficiently meaty so that you have plenty to solve for, and inviting enough for your team to desire to work on. Try to generate multiple questions for every insight and use basic and non-technical language to ensure everyone understands it the same way.

Once this is done, pick the top three statements that the hackathon team agrees on and we'll jumpstart the brainstorming process!

Step 11. Brainstorming

There are many possible ways to brainstorm on your boundary questions. Depending on the dynamics of your hackathon team, here are four brainstorming techniques I recommend:

1. Bounce and Build (B&B)
When most of your team members are comfortable sharing ideas and speaking up, try a B&B.

First, pick a leader. Choose someone who knows how to curate conversations, allowing everyone a fair share of time. This person does not have to be the most senior in the team,

Brainstorming ground rules

Defer judgement
Do not judge each other's ideas. The moment one person starts judging, the quality of the brainstorm session goes downhill.

Quantity over quality
As everyone is trying to go expansive, don't worry about the quality of the ideas for the moment. Keep in mind that not all ideas will go into the eventual build.

Nurture ideas
Listen carefully and help build on each other's ideas.

but avoid choosing the most junior person either, as they run the risk of having the conversation hijacked by the seniors.

Read out your first boundary question: "How might we…?"

Now give everyone three minutes to write down as many ideas as possible. Remember, no discussion at this point. Land one idea per post-it and go for many different ideas, not one big overarching idea. We want quantity over quality at this point.

Once the time is up, pick one team member to share his or her ideas. We do this one idea at a time.

Ask whether any of your team members have similar ideas. Collate all the similar ideas under your boundary questions. Attempt to understand how the ideas on other post-its differ from yours and make sure everyone is heard.

Bounce: After every idea, ask your team members what they think about it. Invite constructive criticism; land them on the post-it note and attach additional post-its as you require. By constructive we mean explaining the context around why you think this idea might or might not work instead of shooting it down with "Your idea is a bad idea".

Build: Now, ask each member to help make your idea a better one. Each member has to start their comment with "Yes, and..." to help build on what you have so far.

Make sure everyone exhausts their post-it notes. The strength of this method is in its openness. Everyone gets a chance to listen and build on each other's ideas – it is the leader's role to ensure air time is fairly distributed to prevent conversation-hogging.

2. Round Robin

If your team has slightly more introverted members who are not so comfortable shouting out their ideas, try Round Robin. The only word of advice I have for anyone attempting this method is: please write neatly!

Sit in a circle. Make sure your next teammate is no more than an arm's length away. Pick the first boundary question your team wants to work on, keeping in mind that we will get around to all three eventually.

Everyone takes a piece of blank A4 paper and starts to scribble one idea pertaining to the boundary question. This should take no more than 90 seconds. If you take more time, you're probably overthinking it.

After 90 seconds, turn the piece of paper over, and pass it on to the person on your right.

Now with the piece of paper you've been handed, take 30 seconds to read through the idea quietly. Then take the next 90 seconds to write down how you can make the idea a better one. Remember to build, not criticise at this point! Start your response with "Yes, and..."

Towards the end you will have four to five fully formed ideas (depending on the number of team members you have) that were thought through carefully by the entire team. Make sure to recognise everyone for their efforts in the co-creation process and give everyone a pat on the back at the end.

3. Ideation Poker
When you need some external stimulus to juice up your brainstorming process, turn to Ideation Poker. This is the opportunity for you to learn from some of the world's best, marrying their success with what you're trying to solve. As this is a more advanced technique, I will go through it in more detail.

Keep in mind, though, that this is a secondary technique, hence use this after B&B or round robin. Do not depend on this as your primary method of idea generation.

Start by selecting a boundary question, e.g. "How might we design a more millennial-relevant credit facility that would suit their lifestyle and needs?"

Each team member nominates the three most innovative companies that they admire. Write each company on a post-it note. Your top choices could be in the tech sector, but media, FMCG, or hospitality companies are all fine. Each team should land at least 10–15 of these companies. Crush all the post-its and put them in the middle of your table.

Pick one post-it from the pile.

Let's say the post-it you picked is Uber. As a team, ask yourselves this question: "If we were Uber, how would we solve this differently?"

Spend the next three minutes discussing what has made Uber such a successful company. Try to identify what we call *signature moments*. Think about interactions that you like, experiences you personally had while dealing with the company of choice. For the case of Uber, you could highlight features such as immediate confirmation, real-time tracking, friendly drivers, and hassle-free payment as examples that are top of mind. Now based on these signature moments, think about how Uber might work on your boundary question.

Hackathon teams going into the ideation stage.

What can you land on? Potentially on ideas such as instant approval, real-time checking of credit application process, personalised account manager services, etc. Keep in mind that there are no right or wrong answers, only fresh inspirations and provocations which lead to better answers to your boundary questions.

Once you feel that you have exhausted all the success factors from the chosen company and merged them successfully with your boundary question, you're now ready to choose another company. Repeat the exercise at least three times.

4. Revolution

If your team members are churning out basic, incremental solutions from other brainstorming methods that are not radical or disruptive enough, you might want to try Revolution as an alternative. This is a secondary technique to help push teams beyond the usual and make sure that they are thoroughly stretched before we conclude the brainstorming process.

Start by choosing a boundary question. As a team, spend five minutes writing down as many existing rules and regulations that govern the current process as possible. Using the earlier example of "How might we design a more millennial-relevant credit facility that would suit their lifestyle and needs?", rules that govern the existing process of credit card application include age limit, issuance of physical card, annual income, bank protocols, creditworthiness checks, etc.

Take each of these rules, and start to break them by asking yourself "What if...?"

- *What if we no longer limit the age of credit card applicants?*

- *What if we no longer need physical cards?*

- *What if we no longer use annual income as a qualifier?*

- *What if we no longer check for creditworthiness?*

When you start to think from this perspective, suddenly the floodgate opens. Go with the flow and you will land on some unexpected ideas.

Spend the next five minutes capturing some of the discussion pointers on post-it notes. Give each rule broken at least 30 seconds to be explored. Some can be fun and insightful; others could be downright ridiculous. Remember, the point in doing this exercise is to find that one, just one "billion dollar" idea, so do not hold back from sharing ideas that may seem absurd at first. Instead, stick to it and ideate away.

Step 12: Conceptualisation

After going through rounds of ideation, your hackathon team will have landed on lots of different ideas. Some of these ideas could be big (such as creating a digital platform) or small (reduce the number of fields required on application forms). What we are aiming to do next is to create a market-ready product or solution, targeted at the needs of your persona group, by synergising the different ideas your team produced during the ideation process.

1. Start by relooking all the ideas you now have. Go through some of the most popular ones, and start to cluster those that your team feels have synergies between them. Give each cluster a high-level name that concisely expresses what the cluster represents.

2. Once you land on several clusters (from six to ten clusters), each team member is now allowed to pick their top two clusters of choice. This is typically based on how disruptive the ideas are and how closely they align with the needs of the customers. Let team members vote using a marker, indicating their choice beside the name of the cluster.

3. After voting, count all the available votes and align on one winning cluster to bring into conceptualisation.

4. With the winning cluster in hand, relook all the post-its again. Imagine if this becomes a product, what would it look like?

5. Take a concept template (below), and start by filling in its value proposition. Based on the

fieldwork done previously, what problems are you trying to resolve? If this product is launched, what type of gains would you anticipate it to bring?

6. Next, sketch out a six-frame storyboard that represents how a customer would use the product. Remember this is from the customer's perspective (we call it the customer journey) and it should clearly illustrate how the "gains" in the

---

Concept Name

Elevator Pitch

Value Proposition

Storyboard

1	2	3

4	5	6

value proposition are made. Try to be as visual with this as possible to fully illustrate the user experience of the proposed product.

7. Give your product a name. Don't worry about whether the choice of name is good – it can be changed anytime. Do not spend too long on this.

8. By now, your team should be able to fill in the elevator pitch easily. This is a two-liner summary of what the product is. Be clear in the way your team expresses it. A good formula is: *"This [your product name], an application that helps you to x, y, z [key features]."*

Once this is done, you have a first version of your solution on hand. Remember to keep the rest of the clusters and not trash them. We will bring the product into experimentation to test if this is what the customer wants. If it fails the customer test, we might scrap it and work on another cluster, so be sure to have more than one cluster to choose from.

This wraps up the human-centred design segment of the hackathon. I hope that through the process, you and your team better understand who your customers are, what they need, and how your designed solution is relevant to them. But how can we be sure that this is what customers in the real world really want? The subsequent chapters on proto-typing will empower you with the right approach, tools and methods to conduct your first customer experiment.

CHAPTER 7

PROTOTYPING I: KICKSTARTING EXPERIMENTATION

WITH A CONCEPT in hand, you are now ready to move into experimentation. For those who fell in love with your concept as you wrote it up, I am sorry to break the news to you: what you perceived as the perfect concept is nothing more than an assumption that was conceived within the four walls of the hackathon room. How can you now move from assumption to a customer-validated product, ready for the upcoming pitch to all your judges and investors? This chapter, on *kickstarting experiments*, and the next chapter, on going *higher-fidelity*, will show you how.

When I say "experiments", some teams might equate that with spending lots of time working out small details, giving their product the perfect name, building code, etc. One team

---

This chapter was co-authored with Darren Yeo.

I saw spent nights creating a clickable digital app of an entire hospital's operations, from queuing to providing healthcare insurance, only to be stumped by the questions from the judges during the Q&A session. Is this something that the patients are looking for? How do you ensure that this supplements the existing workflow of doctors? The judges were not convinced, neither was I.

What you want at this stage is a quick-and-dirty, easy-to-build paper prototype that allows you to experiment with your customers as soon as possible. You'll then be able to channel your learnings into improvements, and subsequently re-test the improved version with another set of customers.

Introducing the identify-build-measure-learn framework. This is, of course, inspired by the hugely successful Lean Start-up methodology designed by Eric Ries. What differs is the additional step of identifying where the riskiest

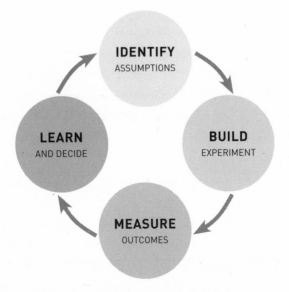

assumptions are made while designing the concept. While this might sound slightly technical, stay patient and walk through the loop once. The moment you close the loop, things will start to make a lot of more sense.

Step 0. Check in

Before we begin the experimentation process, let's do a check-in on the following items covered in the hackathon:

- **Target audience:** Who are the potential users, and what characteristics do they possess?

- **Key insights:** What are some insights that address the underlying tensions faced by the target audience?

- **Concept:** What is the summary of the concept? Why should your customer buy it?

Craft a succinct sentence for each item that can be written on a post-it. This is a simple exercise to assess the level of clarity you have about the topic you are working on.

Step 1. IDENTIFY your riskiest assumptions

Every concept comes with a bag of assumptions. The more novel the concept, the more assumptions it carries. So, you might ask, what exactly is an assumption?

Supposing your hackathon team is thinking of introducing a digital bank in a new market, what you are assuming could potentially be:

1. *Your target audience has access to a stable internet connection to use your proposed digital services.*

2. *Your target audience feels safe transacting online.*

3. *Your target audience has sufficient savings to open a bank account.*

4. *Revenue generated is sufficient to sustain the operation of the digital bank.*

5. *Your back-end infrastructure can support the front-end operation of a digital bank.*

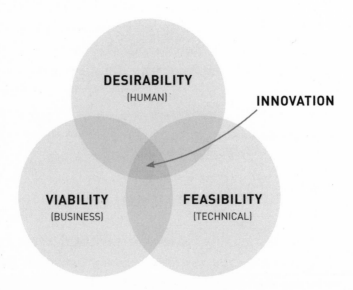

All the above assumptions are valid and should be addressed. Assumptions 1, 2 and 3 relate to *desirability*; 4 is what we call a *business viability* assumption, while 5 is an example of a *technical feasibility* assumption.

At this point, we are particularly interested in desirability, and in identifying which of our assumptions is the riskiest, i.e. the one that is most likely to cause our concept to fail. By addressing it, we will uncover a new set of truths, which will either affirm the validity of our concept, or cause a radical shift in how we proceed. To identify your riskiest assumption:

1. **Unbundle:** First, work out an end-to-end process map of your concept, then review each step to tease out your underlying assumptions. Write each assumption on a post-it.

2. **Cluster:** Cluster the assumptions under their relevant heading – desirability, viability or feasibility. Move the assumptions about desirability to top priority, and leave the other assumptions aside for now.

3. **Compare:** Arrange the desirability assumptions in order of urgency, starting from "No action required" to "We need to test this now!"

4. **Decide:** When you have all your desirability assumptions lined up in order, you'll be able to see which is the riskiest one among them, the one that needs to be tested before all the rest.

Step 2. BUILD your experiment

Now that you have identified the riskiest assumption, we are ready to experiment and to produce a first working prototype. Prototypes give our audience a glimpse of how our concept will benefit them and fulfil their needs. They can be low-fidelity, mid-fidelity or high-fidelity.

- **Low-fidelity prototypes** are paper-based, non-clickable, with little to no real text, no design, and placeholders for all buttons and controls. In some instances, paper-based prototypes can also be digitised via software such as Powerpoint slides with no additional content or details.

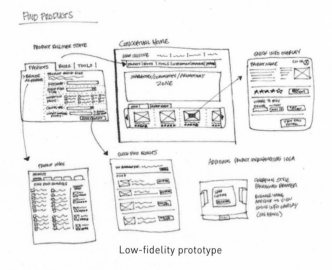

Low-fidelity prototype

- **Mid-fidelity prototypes** are typically digital and build on one of the many prototyping software. They should come with almost all real text, with the actual User Interface (UI) pretty much fleshed out, allowing customers to understand the prototype with little intervention required. The prototype should also receive some basic design treatment in order to look more complete.

Mid-fidelity prototype

- **High-fidelity prototypes** basically look and feel the same as the supposed finished product. All text is real, all media elements work, and controls are in good order. The only reason why it is still considered a prototype is its lack of actual functionality. Once you plug in the right code and databases or APIs, you are good to go.

High-fidelity prototype

For the purpose of a hackathon, a mid-fidelity prototype almost always suffices. In rare instances where the team has some real UI talent, high-fidelity could be achieved but it is never a must to do so.

Given that this is your team's first experiment, aim for low-fidelity. As long as your sketches allow you to tell the story of your concept, that's good enough!

For example, if your concept is a digital one, think about what are the key screens that would allow you to test if your riskiest assumption is true or false. Going back to the digital banking app, if your assumption is *"Your target audience feel safe transacting online"*, draw up a few screens that show how a particular transaction is done via your app. With this, you will be able to communicate to your customers on the transaction and test how safe they feel about transacting online.

Be creative about how you present your paper prototype. You can simulate screenflow or interactivity by folding a long piece of paper, with each fold revealing a key screen. Here are a few other techniques that you could consider using to experiment with your low-fidelity prototype:

- **Storyboarding** is a common tool used by animators to show movement and largely similar to the above process of drawing up keyframes to test the riskiest assumptions you have.

- **Role-playing** is another dimension of storyboarding. Rather than drawing out frames, team

Working out key screens in a prototype

members can act out how the transaction might occur. Plan your story script, and ensure that you address the assumption. Bonus: capture your role-play on your smart devices and share it with more people to capture feedback!

- **Do-it-yourself** is a smart technique that disguises automated actions with manual human effort. What does this mean? If you are trying to test if the customer wants a bill payment option on your proposed digital banking app, allow them to click on your low-fidelity prototype. Once they click on that, manually proceed to the bill payment counter to help your customer pay the bill. Ask them for feedback as they experience the "app-enabled" bill payment system. This removes the need to hardwire the entire bill payment option onto the app and allows us to test if the option is desired by the customer with minimal to no investment required.

The above recommended techniques are some of the most commonly used ones in hackathons. While there are plenty more out there, as a rule of thumb I would recommend that your team complete your first experiment under three hours, with a budget of $3, and a maximum involvement of three team members. The "triple three" will allow you to get something done quickly, so you don't get bogged down with producing mid- or high-fidelity prototypes in the beginning.

Step 3. MEASURE outcomes

With your riskiest assumption on hand and your experiment built, you are now ready to run your experiment! But before that, we will need to help you define what success looks like. What you need is a hypothesis, one that helps you validate assumption into fact. Brant Cooper wrote a simple function in his book, *Lean Entrepreneur*, and that is the exact one we will use for this purpose.

> *"If we do X, Y% of people will behave in way Z."*

Hypothesis explained: X is the design of the experiment, Y is the target metric and Z is the response of the customer.

- **Design of experiment:** Basically what you wanted to test. Based on the earlier mentioned do-it-yourself experiment, it would be: "If we enable bill payment on the digital banking app.."

- **Target Metric:** The success rate you are aiming for to "prove" the assumption to be true. I use the word "prove" as the number here can be quite fluid depending on the experiment you conduct. From my experience, if you are running a face-to-face experiment to elaborate on your storyboard or roleplay, chances are the success rate is very high. In these instances, gun for at least 80% success rate. Generally speaking, the lesser the intervention, the lower the success rate. If you blast an email out to all your customers to test if they are interested, expect a low response rate. In this instance I would say 20% could already be deemed successful. Hence, judge what you are experimenting and make the judgement to adjust your target metric accordingly. To expand on the first hypothesis: "If we enable bill payment on the digital banking app, 80% of the people will..."

- **Customer's response:** How the customer responds to the design of the experiment. If you are out there to test if they would use the bill payment function after you demonstrate it, how would you gauge if they would actually use it? They might say yes quite easily as talk is cheap. But how about getting them to put their contact information down to sign up as a beta tester? Or pledging a small sum to help accelerate the development of the product? These are all forms of "currency exchange" as articulated by Brant Cooper and will be further elaborated on in the

What happens if you don't experiment?

Originally shared by Jillian David via Twitter in July 2017, this photo shows the actual product sample of Aquaria Pasadena Pool Float in white. At first glance the luxuriously soft marbleised design looks oddly familiar. On closer inspection, it looks exactly like a sanitary pad. In Jillian's words: "Focus group. This could have been avoided with one focus group (of women)." This is why you should never underestimate the power of experimenting with your customers.

next chapter as we move into higher-fidelity. What currency do you want to exchange with your customer? A first draft of our full hypothesis for the bill payment feature could look potentially like this: *"If we enable bill payment on the digital banking app, 80% of the people will opt-in to this function once it is available."*

Now you are all set to go out there to run your experiment! Before you head out, remember to prepare a short discussion guide to ask your customers some relevant questions. The fieldwork tips we gave for Chapter 5 are still applicable here. In addition, if you are doing UX (User Experience) tests, pick people who are currently in a stationary position, such as those standing on a bus/train or those sitting in a cafe.

There are three parts to every engagement with a customer:

1. First, give a quick introduction as to what you are trying to do. Ask for permission to proceed.

2. Second, share the experiment. Explain and elaborate as required.

3. Lastly, ask for feedback. How did they find your concept? What can you do to improve?

Step 4. LEARN and decide

How many customers did you share your experiments with? For your first paper prototype, aim to share it with at least seven customers within the same persona type. Once done, you are ready to learn from the experiment and to proceed to decision making. After running seven experiments, take stock:

- **Pivot:** If your success rate is less than 20% for an experiment with 80% as the target success rate (thus suggesting lack of customer desirability), consider pivoting. This means looking for another concept to test. However, I do not recommend pivoting immediately. Why not run your experiment one more time? If the low success rate persists, then perhaps something is really off and you are better off pivoting.

- **Iterate:** This is one of the most common outcomes of experimenting. If your success rate is anywhere from 20% to 80%, look at the feedback captured to better understand what you can learn, and how you can improve. Keep improving, tweaking and making your concept better to help you cross the 80% mark.

- **Persevere:** Once you have crossed the 80% mark, look at how can you experiment with a larger sample size (e.g. 20 customers) to see if your assumption still holds true. If you are still hitting above 80% consistently, you are good. Time to pick another assumption or go higher-fidelity.

CHAPTER 8

PROTOTYPING II:
GOING HIGHER-FIDELITY

AFTER PUTTING pen to paper by sketching up your low-fidelity prototype, you and your team should have learnt to better appreciate the value of customer feedback. As you concretise your concept and gain greater confidence on its desirability, you are now ready to scale. This is the step that differentiates the winning concepts from the ones that will go down the path of mediocrity.

How do you know you are ready to move to higher-fidelity? Simple. Your concepts should have gone through several iteration loops, with their basic assumptions tested. Your customers should have given you positive feedback and built on your concepts, and you are feeling confident about it. Remember, start low-fidelity and slowly move upwards. If you don't know how to appreciate low-fidelity prototypes, go back to Chapter 8. Only when that is done are you ready to move to higher-fidelity.

Why a higher-fidelity prototype?

Going higher-fidelity means that you have moved out of the initial testing phase and are ready to scale. Ideally once you go into mid-fidelity, very minimal intervention will be required for your customers to understand what your team's concept is all about. When you are at high fidelity, it should be as good as a complete product, so zero intervention is required.

With the help of some of the prototyping tools below, you can reach thousands of people within a short span of time, something your low-fidelity prototype couldn't deliver. Hackathon teams now also have unprecedented access to online social media advertising, which their predecessors didn't have. With Facebook advertisements starting as low as US$5, I can safely say that we are in the golden age of digital experiments. Much of what we are going to cover would have been inconceivable just ten years ago, or would have cost us a lot more.

Currency of exchange

As mentioned in the previous chapter, there is a systematic way for us to capture feedback from the customers we are interviewing. Brant Cooper calls this the currency of exchange between the proposed product (your hackathon concept) and the customer. In the real world, we have real currencies. Users pay you money to use your product. But in the world of prototyping, how might they "pay" to indicate their interest? Their expression of interest could range from saying "I like it" to showing real commitment towards your concept. I have summarised the various type of currencies into five categories:

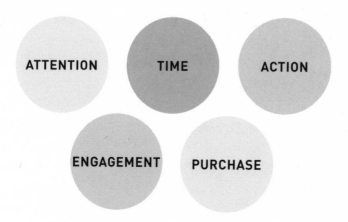

1. **Attention**: Capturing the attention of your customer is in itself an achievement. We can measure this in several increments. Did people stop when you approached them with your prototype? Did they agree to be interviewed? For online experiments, did someone click on the "read more" of your advertisement? Did you get a click-through to your website? Given the huge amount of information we are bombarded with each day, merely being able to capture someone's attention is a first step in the right direction. We are all guilty of carelessly flicking through our newsfeed sometimes, just to pass time. But what really captures our attention? Very little, so the content that you did retain must have done something right.

2. **Time**: Now that you've gotten your customer to stop and listen, or to click through to your website, the next stronger currency would be to give you their time. Did your customer walk away after listening to the introduction? Did your customer drop off halfway while reading the introduction? How much time your customer spent with you is an indicator of the hackathon concept's desirability. If they find your concept of interest, they would be compelled to find out more.

3. **Action**: Now that you have customers stopping by, and willing to spend time with you, getting some pro-active action out of them would be the next currency we want to pursue. It does not have to be very complex. Getting them to sign their name in support if you are running the experiment in person, or sharing the link of your website on their Facebook or Instagram page would be amazing.

4. **Engagement**: What we are gunning for is an opportunity for future engagements. Instead of simply getting their name and contact number, there are several questions we typically ask, e.g. "Do you want to be a beta tester when the final product is launched? If yes, please leave your name and contact information." Questions like these allow us to capture their personal information with the understanding that it will be used

for future engagements. If you really do so in the future, they won't be caught off-guard.

5. **Purchase**: After confirming their interest to be further engaged, the next and highest level of currency you could exchange with your customers is the real world currency: cash. After several successful attempts at getting people to sign up as beta testers, you might want to stretch your experiment further. In this kickstarter-style exchange of currency, they are to pledge real money to be the first to get this particular product when it hits the market. Be ready, though, as your customers may ask you for details such as launch dates, price tiers, etc., once you start to charge. If they are willing to pay, bingo! Your concept is hotly anticipated and you should seriously think about launching it.

Creating the digital prototype

There are several experiments you can run once you get to mid-fidelity. But before that, we need to actually build the mid-fidelity prototype. How do you find a prototyping tool that suits your needs? Based on my own experience developing prototypes, I've summarised the selection process to five basic criteria:

1. **Cost**: Given that most hackathon teams are formed on an ad-hoc basis, you wouldn't need

access to these platforms for more than five days. The good news is, most of the tools out there offer up to 15 days of free trial, so you don't have to spend a cent on them! However, do note that there are some limitations when it comes to the trial version. A nightmare scenario I've seen is when a team chose the wrong tool and the final prototype they presented had a big "TRIAL VER-SION" watermark. It was not only distracting, but embarrassing for the team, so be very careful.

2. **Learning curve:** Basically how long it takes for the user to learn the tool and deliver a prototype. In a hackathon setting, timing is crucial. Go for tools that are simple and easy to use, and avoid those that are cumbersome. This is particularly important for those teams that have no UI/UX designers. You will need to find a platform that has many ready-made components so that you can drag, drop and adjust, rather than starting from scratch.

3. **Platform**: Are you designing for mobile, desktop, tablet or even wearables? There is an increasing trend for hackathon teams to go mobile-native, so that might be a good starting point. Just keep in mind that developing for multiple platforms can be hugely time-wasting so I would advise your team to think it through before even starting work.

Creating a digital prototype

4. **Fidelity:** As explained in the previous chapter, fidelity is about the details. If you are just aiming to demonstrate simple interactions, pick a tool that will help you achieve that. If you are aiming for slick transitions and a full product experience, make sure the tool you pick has the functionality to support that.

5. **Sharing:** In this instance, sharing is about giving multiple users access to support the development of the prototype. In a hackathon, you will typically work in pairs to help expedite the prototype creation process. Having an additional pair of hands is always useful as I have seen more than one instance where the sole designer fell sick and the rest of the team either did not have access or didn't know where to start. But note that not all platforms allow multiple users, so this is another factor to consider.

Based on the above criteria, here are four of the best prototyping tools you can use:

- **Powerpoint:** There are two immediate uses for Microsoft Powerpoint in a hackathon. Firstly, use it to digitise your sketches by snapping photos and arranging them on Powerpoint. This adds a layer of realism to your sketches and allows basic interactivity between screens. The second is that you can utilise the basic vector shapes, gradient fills and transitions to create a prototype within 15–20 minutes. It is quicker than any of the other platforms as we are all super familiar with good old Powerpoint.

- **Proto.io:** Proto.io is a cross-platform prototyping tool. Beyond the basic ability to design an app quickly, it also comes with more advanced features such as "screen recording" to enable collection of feedback. Another highlight is that it breaks down technical jargon into simple layman language. For example, the "swipe left, swipe right" selection method is simply known as "Tinder". The learning curve is hence shorter, allowing you to more quickly get into the field and test out your mid-fidelity prototype.

- **Mockplus:** The basic version of Mockplus comes with 200 templated components, while the paid version comes with an additional 3000 icons to make sure that you never have to look elsewhere. One of the reasons we love Mockplus is its support for quick testing and experimentation. Once your prototype is done, generate a QR code and

Prototyping Tools Compared

	Powerpoint	Proto.io	Mockplus	Marvel
Cost	Free (existing software) or US$99.99 per year	Free for 15 days or US$24 per month	Free for basic version or US$79 per user per year	Free for basic or US$14 per month
Learning curve	*****	**	****	****
Platform	**	****	*****	****
Fidelity	*	***	***	****
Sharing	*	**	**	****
Conclusion	Basic, low-fidelity but quick	Pricier option with useful advanced options	Fuss-free and quick but not built for collaboration	Well-priced, consistent performer

that's all you need to bring. Ask your respondents to scan the QR, and they instantly have your prototype interface on their own mobile phone. Alternatively, you can also generate a web link and disseminate it to everyone in your network for testing. Sweet.

- **Marvel:** Marvel is one of the most established and widely used prototyping tools right now. Chances are, if you ask ten hackathon teams what they are using, half of them would say Marvel. The exciting case studies of how Marks & Spencer and Deliveroo delivered real value using Marvel make a strong case for using this tested and proven tool. One of the highlights of Marvel is that it even supports the Apple watch, so if you are thinking of leveraging wearables as part of your prototyping process, Marvel is the way to go.

Landing page experiments

In its purest form, a landing page is a standalone web page that your visitor lands on after clicking on the given link to your website. In the world of hackathons, we use this as a tool to test and validate our concept at scale, accumulate feedback from a larger audience and as an avenue for currency exchange.

The key reason why we use a landing page is because it is simple, concise, and quick to create. Key items to include in your landing page are a concept summary, an introduction of key features and a walkthrough of the user interface. Towards the end of the page, you will be seeking to exchange a currency with the visitor. For landing page experiments, I would seek *engagement* as the currency of exchange, with a sign-up form to gauge interest.

A mobile app landing page template from Wix.com

Top tip: There are many site creation tools out there, but I generally recommend Wix, Strikingly and Unbounce as top choices. They all have a wide range of templates to choose from. Creating a landing page shouldn't take more than an hour of your time.

Social media advertising

Earlier I mentioned that we are in the golden age of online advertising, and here you will see why. Just a decade ago, buying online ad space was something reserved for those with serious advertising budgets. But now, everyone and anyone, including hackathon teams, can buy themselves some highly targeted advertisements with a small fee. I will use Facebook ads as an example, but other social media channels such as Instagram, Snapchat and LinkedIn work in a similar fashion.

Step 1. Create a Facebook page: Start by creating a page for your hackathon concept. Depending on the nature of your concept, it can either be a company page or a product page.

Step 2. Pick an objective: Go into Facebook's ad manager, and depending on what you want to achieve and the currency you want to exchange with your users, pick one of the 15 options available. For example, if you are seeking click-throughs to your landing page, choose "Increase conversions on your website".

What's your marketing objective?		
Awareness	**Consideration**	**Conversion**
Boost your posts	Send people to a destination on or off Facebook	Increase conversions on your website
Promote your Page	Get installs of your app	Increase engagement in your app
Reach people near your business	Raise attendance at your event	Get people to claim your offer
Increase Brand Awareness	Get video views	Promote a product catalogue
Increase your reach	Collect leads for your business	Get people to visit your shops

Step 3. Defining your audience: Selecting your audience is where Facebook shines. You get a wide range of options to pick from here, starting from location, age and gender, to languages, interest, behaviours and connections. Review your target customers' personas to help you choose accordingly. Facebook will then be able to provide you with an estimated daily reach based on your selection.

Step 4. Budget and time: Once that is done, you will be redirected to the budget and schedule page. Depending on how much budget you have, you can input accordingly. Your budget can go as low as S$10 a day but keep in mind that you only have half a day to run your ad, so to maximise your reach, I would recommend stretching the daily budget to the highest possible to increase exposure. Next, pick a start and end date, depending on how long you want your ad to run.

Step 5. Create your advert: Facebook currently offers five different advertisement types, ranging from carousel mode (where there are two or more scrollable images/videos) to single image, single video, slideshow and the new canvas mode, where you get to combine images and videos to tell a compelling story.

How ads made *The 4-Hour Workweek* a number one bestseller

Tim Ferriss came up with six potential titles for his book, including *Broadband and White Sand*, *Millionaire Chameleon* and *The 4-Hour Workweek*, and developed a Google Adwords campaign for each. He was interested to see which sponsored post would be clicked on the most, knowing that he would be going up against more than 200,000 titles published in USA each year. By the end of the week-long Google Adwords experiment, and for less than US$200, *The 4-Hour Workweek* had a much better clickthrough rate by far, so he went ahead with that title. The book went one to become a number one bestseller according to both the *New York Times* and the *Wall Street Journal*.

Step 6. Ad placement: Once the ad has been created, you can choose where you want to ads to appear on Facebook and Facebook's sister application, Instagram. Some options you get to choose from include the mobile news feed, desktop news feed and Instagram ads.

Facebook Desktop and Mobile

Instagram Mobile

Step 7. Payment: Click on the Place Order button at the bottom right corner and Facebook will proceed with a short review before publishing the advertisement. My previous ad took two to three hours to get through the review, so make sure you have some lead time to allow for that.

CHAPTER 9

FACILITATION AND MENTORSHIP

HACKATHONS ARE action-oriented, fast-paced, and often emotionally charged. In such an environment, we expect participants to feel lost and at times helpless. That's the time to call on the facilitators to mentor the participants. This chapter lays out the expectations around how facilitators should act and mentor during hackathons, and shares some of the most useful tools we have used in different situations.

Who are the facilitators?

There are two types of facilitators that participants will typically meet at a hackathon: the main facilitators, typically one or two of them; and table facilitators, who are assigned to every two to three teams. Each of them performs a particular role:

The main facilitator(s)

The main facilitators are like the anchors of the room, the ones who have absolute control throughout the course of the hackathon. They are typically quite loud, with the ability to command the attention and respect of the participants.

Main facilitators also need to have a complete understanding and mastery of the presentation content. Why is that useful? I once had a projector crisis where the bulb of the projector broke five minutes into the hackathon and we had to present everything off-hand. This happens, and you should be ready for it. Also, be ready for all sorts of questions as there might be people who will be challenging why we are doing certain activities.

Tip: Pick the best speaker in your team for this role. In the corporate context, someone mid-senior level is preferred as they command a suitable level of respect from the audience.

Main facilitator

Choosing a junior person might undermine what you are trying to get done at a hackathon as they might be challenged unnecessarily at times. That said, some of the juniors I have met possess such a great amount of energy and are the obvious choice for the role. In such instances, allow a senior to kickstart the day and set the stage, then hand over to the junior. This ensures the right endorsement is given and sets up the facilitator for success.

The table facilitators

Table facilitators should be well equipped with the ability to decipher the facial expressions of participants. The same applies for the main facilitators, but as much as the main facilitators want to, they cannot maintain constant eye contact with each and every one of the participants. They are also more concerned with the big picture and less with the individuals.

This is where table facilitators shine and step in to be the observant one. Ideally, there should be one table facilitator for every 15–20 participants. These participants, from across two to three groups, should always be within your line of sight. Whenever you observe participants looking puzzled, be proactive in clarifying what exactly they don't understand. This ensures that participants feel that they are well taken care of.

Table facilitators should also be approachable. Being around, akin to the management principle of Management By Walking Around (MBWA), helps establish visibility and promotes exchanges between table facilitators and participants.

Table facilitators are also expected to sit down with their teams, get their hands dirty and help bring their teams to a desired level of output. Whenever necessary, correct the team if they are following the wrong methodology. Participants also need validation on the ideas they have generated, and facilitators should be able to give feedback on whether these ideas are sufficiently groundbreaking.

One common problem that hackathon teams face is that everyone is opinionated and sometimes no one is willing to budge. As a table facilitator, if you sense that there is one individual who is stopping the team from moving on, use anonymous voting. Each team member gets a post-it and writes their choice down. Get them to crush their post-its and hand them in to you. You then look through all the post-its and reveal the winning idea. No one is then allowed to dwell on the losing idea(s) any further.

On planning

The main facilitators have a huge responsibility to drive the success of the hackathon. Being the "face" of the event, your hackers/audience/judges will all be looking at you to deliver instructions in a succinct and eloquent way, set the tone of the event in an energetic way, and most importantly, engage them.

Here is a planning tool that has helped us deliver success over and over again. I hope that it can do the same for you. For each activity you run, ask yourself these questions:

- **What is this activity?** What is a clear name you can use to illustrate the activity? Names you choose should be self-explanatory; if they aren't, think of something else.

- **When are you doing it?** E.g. which part of the day? Special attention should be given to after-lunch hours, when food coma sets in. Try not to do any long lecture-type sharing after meals. Aim for something hands-on to keep the participants awake.

- **What materials and resources do you need?** For each activity, do you need additional paper, markers, post-its, or additional time to set up (if you're putting things up on the wall)? Remember to account for these turnaround times as time adds up and you might be behind by 30 minutes to an hour before you realise it.

- **Why are you doing it?** What is the intention behind this activity? Be brutal and crystal clear. Depending on what you're hacking on, not all activities need to be done. You need to be selective over your choice of activities and the why becomes especially important.

- **How are you doing it?** Lay out the step-by-step instructions. Do not assume that all hacks are the same. Make an additional effort to contextualise what you're trying to do – your participants will thank you for it. You will also be glad when they are able to follow on as planned.

- **What are the outputs and takeaways?** This is the most important of all the questions above. Your output and takeaways should be linked to why you are doing the next activity. There shouldn't be any activity that you are doing just for the sake of doing it. If any of these exist or if you simply find it hard to weave them back to the larger narrative, it's time to kill the activity and move on to something else

More tips for main facilitators:

- We typically plan our time in five-minute blocks. Some might feel that this is over-planning, but such detailed plans work especially well for new facilitators as they lack the experience to gauge the required time for each activity.

- If a certain activity ends earlier than expected, experienced facilitators know how to ad-lib their way through the remaining time. This means speaking spontaneously. A good question to throw at participants is "How are you feeling so far?" and pick one or two hackers to have a conversation with. Or simply give them the time to clarify any questions that they might have.

- Be genuine with your audience, e.g. by sharing with them that they may need to work overtime because of certain parts overrunning. Of course, this can be difficult as some may feel that the hackathon is not well managed, but remember that honesty is always the best policy.

On arguments

It is natural for hackathon teams to occasionally be engulfed in an argument. In any environment as pressuring as a hackathon, emotions tend to run high very easily. To us, this is actually a good sign as it shows that the participants are vested in the work they are doing. Only interested participants would bother to argue as they care about the outputs. Disengaged participants wouldn't bother arguing; they simply switch off.

But how can we as facilitators help them get past the arguments? I often encourage them to take the argument outside the hackathon room, by that I mean testing their respective beliefs with actual customers (see Chapter 6).

Beyond that, we would also like to teach them a life skill – one that will allow them to give better feedback to their teammates. Introducing "Feedback as a gift", a model developed by Stanford academic Carole Robin. Below is a new interpretation of the seven points made by Robin, with hackathons as the context:

Hackathon teams can be guided to overcome
arguments and produce great work

- **Do it early:** Instead of allowing the unhappiness
  and misalignment to pass, address the issue the
  soonest possible. Remember, it is alright to be
  the dumb person in the room and ask, "What did
  that mean? Why do you think it is a good idea?
  What do you mean by that?" The longer it drags,
  the more disruptive it is to the team, and painful
  for the person on the receiving end.

- **Avoid shaming:** Negative feedback can cause the
  recipient to feel shame or "lose face", particularly in Asia. Remember that no idea is stupid. Be
  careful around how you approach this topic and
  be extra sensitive. Instead of saying someone's
  idea is no good or inferior, make an additional
  effort to explain why the other method is a better
  one.

- **Focus on behaviour:** If your team is held up by a disruptive member, instead of calling the person out, focus on their behaviours that you deem disruptive. If the disruption is caused by a non-participative teammate (often seen at corporate hackathons), ask each member for contributions. The most important point here is fairness – everyone should be doing a task of similar intensity. If that doesn't work, get a table facilitator in to help distribute the work effectively.

- **Stay on your side of the net:** Building on the above point, instead of harping on "You did not do this!" or "You are at fault!" when disagreement happens, avoid having "you" in the statements, as argued by Robin. Focus on the facts and the impact of the actions. "I believe this can be better done" or "I recommend that we try another method" can be good starting points.

- **Be generous:** Always remember that no one comes to a hackathon with bad intentions. We are all here to learn, grow and do something great. With that in mind, think about how you can help each other achieve that. A simple way is to be genuine and generous with your praise. If your teammate did something amazing, say so. What you will realise is that it bonds the team and helps defuse arguments between participants.

- **State your intent:** Be clear with what are you trying to achieve. In a situation of conflict between team members, beating around the bush is not going to help. Go straight to the point, and show that what you're trying to get done helps him/her too. Show that you care. If that is difficult, your table facilitator is there to help.

- **Practise:** It can be hard to action on all of the above gifting methods, and we recognise that. However, as Robin correctly points out, we don't get better by not doing it. Keep giving feedback, keep making mistakes and keep getting better – this is how we learn in general and the same applies for giving feedback. Exercise your feed-back muscles!

Advanced facilitation: Business mentorship

While it is important for all facilitators to learn and under-stand the facilitation skills required to run a hackathon, a more experienced group of them should form the core busi-ness mentoring team for the end of Day 2 to provide business mentorship for the teams. During this segment, the hacka-thon teams take turns to give the business mentorship group an update of their progress.

The business mentoring group should be staffed by the most senior facilitators in the team. Actual experts from the busi-nesses could also be invited, depending on their availability, to give advice. As this is less formal than the actual pitch on Day 3, the teams are given ten minutes to give their progress update and, more importantly, introduce their solution. Teams should share their target audience, insights found, concept and initial feedback collected so far.

If you are part of this business mentorship group, you will then give feedback to the participants based on your years of experience interacting with actual customers. If you find that the insights are not well informed or are outright wrong, feel free to challenge them. Also comment on the freshness of the solution – it might be that the solution has already been done by competitors, or has been tested but failed in the past, or is already in the pipeline. If any of the above is true, inform the team and offer suggestions on how they can iterate on the solution.

Also help the teams on the business viability of their solution. If they are pricing it completely wrong, or you see no way they could ever be profitable with their proposed revenue model, share your concerns and offer suggestions.

With basic mistakes rectified, the actual pitches on Day 3 will be of much higher quality. If possible, do one more round of check-in with the teams the next morning to give them another chance to practise their pitch. If there is a second round of business mentoring, get the teams to comply with the five-minute time restriction to make it more real.

CHAPTER 10

PITCHING AND JUDGING

AFTER TWO intense days (and nights) of hacking and rigor-
ous testing, you now have a winning insights-driven concept.
But before declaring victory, remember that you still must
pass the final test. This chapter will guide you through what
a good pitch looks like, so you can convince the judges that
your concept is the winning one.

Elements of a good pitch deck

At this point, I would like to reference Guy Kawasaki's
10/20/30 rule – 10 slides, 20 minutes to present, with font
size 30 points or larger. Highly useful and relevant when
you're pitching to VCs (venture capitalists), but less so for a
hackathon. Here, we go by the rule of thumb of 5/10/15. How
does this work?

- **5 minutes:** In a typical hackathon we run, participants get five minutes to present, plus three minutes for Q&A. The amount of time you get is non-negotiable. Some other hackathons I have attended only gave three minutes to present. Make sure you clarify and ask before getting any work done.

- **10 slides:** Aim for a ten-slide pitch deck. If you follow the earlier point of delivering all your content within five minutes, that gives you thirty seconds a slide effectively – with no hiccups in between. Remember, presentation time is precious, hence you must know exactly why each slide exists and what purpose it serves.

- **15-point font size:** With ten slides as a cap, I have seen many participants try to squeeze as much text onto one page as possible. That's generally bad practice. I advise my participants to keep to font size 15 as the smallest. And these should only be used as subtext and elaboration. Headers should ideally be size 30, as advised by Guy Kawasaki. But also remember that you have additional tools in **bold**, <u>underline</u> and *italics*.

So, you have ten slides to work with – but what do you do with them? On the following pages, I'll sketch out, slide by slide, how to structure your pitch for the best results.

Slide 1: The Introduction

Be bold and kick off with a bang! In a short and concise way, introduce who you are and give a two-liner introduction of your product.

Incorporate your long-term goal and the high-level problem into your introduction. Strive to be as *audacious* as possible to leave an impact. Think about what you want the judges to remember after hearing all the pitches.

Try: "We are X [your team name] and we are here to make Y [problem] a thing of the past. Introducing Z." For example: "We are Team Q-less and we are here to make in-branch queues a thing of the past. Introducing DigiQ, our appoint-ment-scheduling app that gets you a number even before you reach the branch."

Slide 2: The Problem

For this slide, focus on answering two questions. Who are your target customers? And what is the problem you are trying to solve? This should be grounded in research and validated by the fieldwork that your team has done.

Think about how you can make the judges say, "Ouch, I feel that problem too!" Bring back your persona and most importantly, make the problem relatable. Use time, numbers, days, etc., to illustrate how much of a pain it is. If you see people cringing or nodding, you are on the right track. This slide is super important as it helps you build up to the solution.

Other ways of presenting the problem include more interactive approaches such as role-playing, or showing a video of the existing process to illustrate the pain involved.

What is the problem?

 Problem 1 : Insights-based pain point collected during fieldwork

 Problem 2 :

CONCLUSION:
The BIG takeaway summarised into a single sentence.

Slide 3: The Solution

Once you have established the pain, jump straight into how you are going to solve it. Share with your audience the key value proposition.

Within the value proposition, you should reiterate the problem, how your solution has alleviated the pain, and any other gains from using your solution.

Writing your value proposition is a mixture of art and science. Uber's key value proposition is "Tap the app, get a ride", and supplemented by "Uber is the smartest way to get around. One tap and a car comes directly to you. Your driver knows exactly where to go, and payment is completely cashless." Think about what that means for your solution.

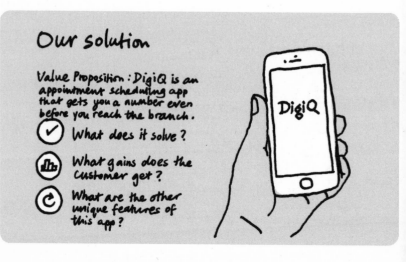

Slide 4: The Demo

Use the mid/high-fidelity prototype your team created during the prototyping phase to showcase the end-to-end experience your team is proposing. Go touchpoint by touchpoint and elaborate on how your solution alleviates the pain and creates moments of delight within the customer's journey. This reinforces the improved (or brand new) experience your team wants to provide.

Instead of showing your prototype and clicking through the screens on the spot, use Quicktime's screen recording function (available on most Mac machines). You can speed up the video or trim it to suit your presenter's talking speed. This is highly recommended as technical issues often crop up during demo, derailing the entire presentation.

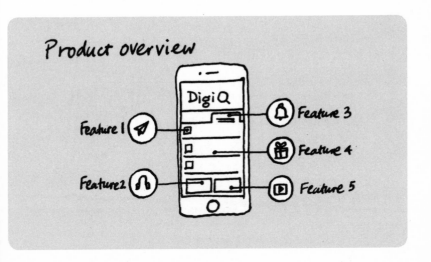

Slide 5: Customer's validation

Reinforce whatever you have said with positive feedback received from customers. What you're trying to do here is show the judges that customers have *validated* your solution, and the solution is desired by them. Reference the experiments you conducted, and the responses you received, to help build your case.

Tip: Numbers always help here. I'm not suggesting that you mix qualitative data with quantitative, but if you have some numbers to back yourself up – flaunt them! One of the most impressive hackathon teams I've seen conducted a landing page experiment and drew more than 2000 likes on Facebook in a short span of ten hours. Such numbers will give the judges confidence that your solution is the right one.

What did customers say?

75% of potential customers are willing to download and try DigiQ.

50% of customers are reminded of DigiQ when they next visit a branch.

90% of customers are willing to recommend DigiQ to a friend.

Slide 6: Market opportunity

With the problem established, solution provided, and customers heard, the next step is to quantify how big the market
opportunity is. Use a pie chart (or any other data visualisation
tool) to help you communicate how big the opportunity is.
Contrasting colors will also help guide the eyes of the judges.

Start by defining the number of potential customers and how
much they typically spend on a similar product today. Your
target is to get the judges excited about the solution from
a business viability standpoint and understand that there is
money to be made here.

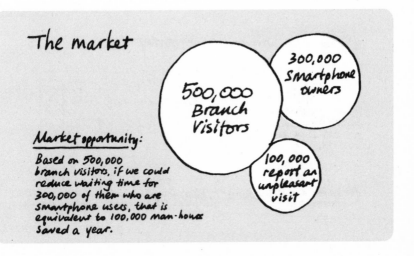

Slide 7: Napkin business case

This slide will dig deeper into the dollars and cents. Focus on answering these three questions:

1. How much will it cost to produce your product?

2. If you sell this to one customer, how much money can you expect to make?

3. How long will it take for you to be profitable?

This slide is the one most frequently picked on, as the judges (often senior stakeholders in corporates or VCs) will have real-world numbers at their fingertips. Keep that in mind, and be ready to justify your estimates. The judges will want to see that your team has put in some serious consideration into making your product profitable.

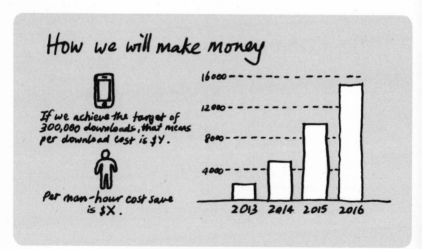

Slide 8: Competitor landscape

List your top five competitors and their value propositions. Compare them against yours to show that your team has identified a gap that hasn't been sufficiently addressed.

If there isn't exactly a gap, your team will almost certainly be asked the question, "How do you differentiate your product from your competitors'?" Your answer could be that you offer an improved experience or a new business model – make sure your team has thought this through prior to the pitch.

Take note that this is not going to be a full-fledged SWOT (Strengths, Weaknesses, Opportunities, Threats) analysis; however, do think of leveraging your strengths, your competitors' weaknesses and the opportunities identified to help differentiate your solution from the rest of the field.

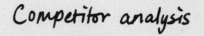

Competitor analysis

DIRECT
Other queuing services apps providing similar services.

INDIRECT
Services in the market that are indirectly providing similar services.

Slide 9: Next steps

The bulk of the convincing should already have been done. What's left is to briefly talk about the next steps. Visualise this as an implementation timeline – what should be done in the next six months, twelve months and beyond? Are there any immediate action points, such as onboarding partners, that your team plans to embark on? It would also be useful to list the new features that you plan to implement in the next couple of years to get the judges excited about your future vision.

This is a good-to-have, so if you are running out of time, this is the slide to fly through.

Next steps

Jan 2018	○	With funding, next step to start development.
Jun 2018	○	UI and UX design.
Dec 2018	○	Commencement of user test.
Feb 2019	○	Pilot rollout.
Apr 2019	○	Iteration and learning.
Aug 2019	○	Linking to back-end database.
Mar 2020	○	All features done and delivered.

Slide 10: Team

And that's all! Use the last slide to wrap up. Run through who is in your team, their contributions, and give everyone a chance to be acknowledged for their hard work. Remember, innovation is a team sport and none of this would have happened without everyone's contribution. Once done, repeat your team name and end off with the punchline you started with.

Our team

JUSTIN
Graphic Designer

LEE
CEO

EMILY
Sales Executive

Some final pitching tips

- **Limit the bullet points to three:** Learn from experienced McKinsey consultants and use the rule of three they swear by. If you are seeking to convince someone, always use three reasons. Not two, not four, but exactly three. This forces you to pick the top three reasons amongst many, and helps you sound more structured and confident.

- **Don't read off your script/slides:** You risk losing eye contact if you start regurgitating every single word you have on your slide, and end up losing your charm as a presenter.

- **Come prepared:** For the three-minute Q&A, be ready for really harsh questions. Think through all the possible questions, and conduct pre-Q&A with someone senior. If visuals help you give a better response, have them in your appendix. Most of my hackathon teams prepare at least 20 questions before they go for the final pitch.

- **Aim for euphoria:** If you achieve a sense of euphoria during your presentation, you probably nailed it. If you don't, fake it – smile widely during the presentation as the positivity on your face will permeate through to your voice and how you deliver the presentation, eventually reaching the judges and leaving a far more positive experience than the one who didn't smile.

- **Natural selection bias:** Judges tend to select concepts that can reach the market first, because they want to monetise these concepts as soon as possible. Even if your full concept can't be implemented in six months, probably some bits of it can. Make sure you highlight these bits.

- **March on:** If tech fails when you are presenting, have a plan B available. Keep in mind that tech hiccups do not warrant a time extension. Therefore, be ready to start even when your deck crashes, leaving you with a black screen. Instead of wasting time, say something. The ever-reliable old-fashioned cue cards, or even a printed script in your back pocket, can come in handy in times like this.

How will your team be judged?

After getting all the pitch preparations done, it is now a good time to shift gears to look at how the judges will be judging. Here are some routines to help organisers get started and get ready for the pitching segment.

Arrange for the judges to come in at least two hours before the final pitch. It is best if the judges fully understand the progress so far, and are fully immersed in the vibes of the hackathon. Brief the judges on the challenge statements, and run them through the typical judging criteria as outlined below. Do note that we typically choose from a mixture of the criteria. Curate a set of judging criteria that best suits the needs of your hackathon.

Judging Form

#	Team/Concept	Comments	Place
1			
2			
3			
4			
5			
6			

Judging Criteria

Relevance to business	Quality of insights	Ambition level	Pitch quality

Criteria 1. Relevance to business problem (or challenge statement)

How is the product/concept solving a pressing business challenge? What fresh perspectives does it bring from the business' standpoint? Regardless of how great the idea is, it must solve a pressing challenge. What the judges are looking for is your understanding of the business. Speak their lingo, make it real for them and get them excited with the money you could make.

But how do you get an understanding if this is the first time you're solving a challenge from this business domain? Start by interviewing anyone in the room who is working on the business itself. Make sure to capture their opinions. Next, make use of the business mentoring session to maximise your understanding of the business.

Tip: If you want to score on this (or any of the other criteria), flag, highlight or bring forward the points to help the judges award you the marks.

Criteria 2. Quality of insights

There are a few things the judges are looking for under this judging criteria. Did your team fully utilise the learnings from the research phase and build on it based on your fieldwork? It is perfectly alright if you want to challenge the findings of the insights document. Be prepared, however, to ground your decision with solid research. Show photos of customer inter-actions, screen captures of experiments and verbatim feed-back to help establish your case. You can further strengthen your case with quantitative data such as Facebook likes, sign-ups and payment received. These will be differentiators that help your team stand out.

Criteria 3. Ambition level

Ambition level is typically where conventional corporate teams fall short. Years of experience inform them of what works and what doesn't, leading to BAU (Business-As-Usual) responses that surprise no one. Hackathons are formed with the exact opposite end in mind. Domain experts are mixed with colleagues from other departments, forming cross-functional teams. These teams are given the mandate to go wild, be creative and impress judges with their innovation. It is definitely most disappointing for teams to produce BAU-type solutions.

What then does success look like? Sparkle in the eyes of the judges who can't wait to bring your concept into the market? Possibly. But I know it is not realistic to ask that of every single hackathon team. The advice I give to all my hack teams is to "reject being ordinary". If the solution sounds reasonable to you, or could have been thought up by any one of you before the hack, try harder. If the solution could be fully implemented within one year, try harder too.

Tip: Look at the existing technology-based solutions, a natural benchmark given the tech focus of most hacks – are you outdoing them? If not, are you even on par? Set yourself up against the best in the world. Quoting the mantra of DBS Innovation Group: Go big or go home!

Criteria 4. Pitch quality

The impression of quality boils down to what the judges see, hear, feel and experience during the five minutes of pitch and three minutes of Q&A. Another key principle I live by is the policy of "no ugly slide". Make sure you have spent some time to think about the aesthetics of your presentation. You don't have to be a graphic designer, but at least keep to one template. Use one consistent set of fonts. All this sounds minor, but when the competition is too close to call, the quality of the pitch itself becomes the tie-breaker.

Another very important aspect of pitch quality is your presenter. Choose the most eloquent person from your team to present. This is not the time nor opportunity for weaker presenters to practise. Have one consistent presenter throughout. If you are incorporating role-play into your presentation, the presenter should ideally stay out of it and allow others to do the role-playing.

Tip: Have a dedicated tech person to look after everything tech. If you are showcasing an app mockup or redirecting the presentation to another page to show a video, make sure all this is well set up prior to the presentation. The tech person should also know how to resolve basic issues such as Powerpoint crashing, restarting the prototyping platform, etc.

One final parting statement I have is that Murphy's Law applies here. Whatever can go wrong, will go wrong. Always carry a printed set of notes with you and have them in your back pocket. You will win extra points from the judges if you have things under control. Good luck and happy pitching!

CHAPTER 11

CONCLUSION

RUNNING A SUCCESSFUL hackathon is very often the first step in creating something great. But all too often, much of the positive energy dissipates from here on and the winning idea eventually falls behind in priority as compared to BAU (Business-As-Usual). Therefore, a deliberate attempt to harness the positive energy is required. In this concluding chapter, I will try to answer all the frequently asked – and often difficult-to-answer – questions coming from both organisers and participants.

From prototype to marketplace

Let's go straight to the point that both the organisers and the winning team are probably thinking now: what's next? First, what do we actually have? The check-list should include a pitch deck, a mid-fidelity prototype, basic data that shows a high-level of customer desirability, and of course a group of passionate people who can't wait to see their concept go into the market. All these are good ingredients for a successful product, but there are some immediate next steps that you need to consider.

Firstly, more experimentation is required. Are you certain that the experiments conducted during the hackathon hold water? Repeat the experiments with more people this time – e.g. expand it to 2–3 times your original sample size. You also want to make sure that constant iteration is being done, in order to constantly improve the quality of your prototype. In the process, insert more actual design assets (like the corporate logo, branding), real text and functionality to bring your prototype from mid-fidelity to high-fidelity. Remember that high-fidelity means the prototype should work like in the real world, the only difference being that it isn't connected to the back-end database.

That said, experimentation shouldn't go on forever. So once the riskiest and most known elements are cleared, we are good to move into closed beta or a pilot launch. What a pilot phase entails is that a small group of early adopters (typically up to 1000) will be recruited to test the end product. At this point, the high-fidelity prototype is linked up to the back-end database, and everything should work as per normal. The beta is called "closed" because it is not open to other customers beyond the chosen early adopters.

By this time, the skillsets required to bring the concept into the market will probably exceed the manpower and technical capabilities of the hackathon team. For example, your subsequent experiments might require a UX specialist to work

A new and refreshed way of working

So far, I have only covered the next steps for the winning team and concept. But what if you didn't win the hackathon? That's a fair question to ask, as 75% of all participants will not win or fall into the top three teams. Does that mean that you have wasted your time? Certainly not!

- In the three-day process, you would have forged a strong bond with your team mates. You experienced ups and downs together, you fought and you listened. This is way more effective a bonding exercise than the typical offsite.

- Remember the human-centred design tools you learnt. These are applicable for any customer-facing role as you now have a structured way and a set of tools to help you better engage your customers.

- Start experimenting! No one can claim that their ideas are perfect without speaking to customers. Keep testing, learning and iterating. Each time you iterate, you come a step closer to the ultimate customer truth you are seeking.

- Lastly, make every presentation you run in the future a pitch. The 5/10/15 principle lives beyond the hackathon and can help you deliver a better presentation every single time.

on the iterations, or someone familiar with the tech stack to work on the closed beta launch. You might also need marketing, branding, naming support to ensure that the product stays consistent with the rest of the company. Hence, knowing who to bring in, when to bring them in and having their commitment towards bringing the post-hackathon prototype into the market is of absolute importance.

We typically circumvent this by inviting the heads of the various departments in as judges. This serves two purposes. If they agree that the prototype is of value to their business, then it shouldn't be difficult to get their commitment towards assigning resources to bring the prototype into the market. By bringing the right senior stakeholders into the room, we also cut short the socialisation process required post-hackathon to convince others that the winning concept is of value.

From a timing perspective, we need to "strike while the iron is hot". Kickstart conversations about bringing the winning concept into the market within the next ten days, otherwise work will pile up and you will lose traction. Aim to run your experiments to clear all the risky and unknown assumptions within eight to twelve weeks, and a closed beta shortly after. So far, the closed beta testing phases I have conducted ranged from three to six months, depending on the scope and number of early adopters. The closed beta should give you a strong business case to unlock funding and push the product into the marketplace.

And that is all I have for you. Let's make hackathons a mainstay of the business world!

ACKNOWLEDGEMENTS

EVEN AFTER I finished writing *Hackathons Unboxed*, the possibility of being a published book author still seemed so surreal. The whole book project came about during my 2016 December vacation in Bali. Wondering what would make 2017 an awesome year, I set myself the challenge of writing a book, and the rest is history.

This book would not have been possible without the support of Chun Yuan. Thanks CY, for believing that I could finish the book project, and putting up with my last-minute editing requests. Since our undergraduate days, I've known that you are someone I can always depend on, and the best editor I could ever ask for.

I would also like to express my gratitude to Melvin and Justin from Marshall Cavendish, who saw the potential in this book project. Your support and validation mean a lot to me – an unknown author with no track record.

Thanks Anthony, for the book cover design that I fell in love with immediately. Your designs never cease to amaze me every single time.

Thanks Neal, for being not only a supporter, but also an advocate of this book project. Your endorsement was instrumental in helping me getting the book published. Your foreword set the stage and the tone of this book. I look forward to your upcoming book, *Jungle Innovation.*

Thanks Darren, for accepting my invite to co-write Chapter 7. Your insights and perspectives made this book a much better one.

Thank you, DBS Bank. The vision of Piyush Gupta, David Gledhill, Paul Cobban, Neal Cross, Bidyut Dumra and Mark Evans set the strategic directions and gave the entire DBS Innovation Group, including myself, an opportunity to bring the hackathon methodology to the 22,000-person startup.

Lastly, thank you everyone who participated in the workshops and hackathons I conducted. Your patience, feedback and comments allow me to improve every single time.

ABOUT THE AUTHOR

ALVIN CHIA is the Innovation Program Lead of DBS Bank, and a seasoned hacker. His tenure in DBS has seen him conducting more than 50 hackathons and workshops across the region, solving business challenges such as digitisation and new product development.

Prior to DBS, Alvin consulted for the largest independent innovation consulting company, serving top-tier clients such as InterContinental Hotels Group (IHG), GlaxoSmithKline (GSK) and Unilever.

Outside of work, Alvin lectures actively as adjunct faculty and writes for the business and leadership verticals of the *Huffington Post*.

Contact Alvin via the *Hackathons Unboxed* website:
www.hackathonsunboxed.com